Contents

BAKED ASPARAGUS WITH BALSAMIC BUTTER SAUCE ....
EASY MEXICAN CASSEROLE 6
ITALIAN BREADED PORK CHOPS 7
UNBELIEVABLE CHICKEN 7
LEMON GARLIC TILAPIA 8
HUMMUS 9
CREAM CORN LIKE NO OTHER 9
ORZO WITH PARMESAN AND BASIL 10
SPAGHETTI CARBONARA 10
TACO PIE 11
APPLE STRUDEL MUFFINS 12
SPANISH RICE 13
BAKED CHICKEN NUGGETS 13
SAUTEED APPLES 14
A GOOD EASY GARLIC CHICKEN 14
EASY TUNA CASSEROLE 15
FRENCH TOAST CASSEROLE 15
SOUR CREAM PORK CHOPS 16
SLOW COOKER LEMON GARLIC CHICKEN 17
GREEK CHICKEN PASTA 17
VEGETARIAN CHICKPEA SANDWICH FILLING 18
SPICY BEAN SALSA 19
KEY WEST CHICKEN 19
QUICK CHICKEN PICCATA 20
BANANA OAT MUFFINS 21
AMAZING CHICKEN 21
RED LENTIL CURRY 22
UNSTUFFED CABBAGE ROLL 22
BEEF BARLEY VEGETABLE SOUP 23
ASIAN BEEF WITH SNOW PEAS 24
TENDER ITALIAN BAKED CHICKEN 24
BOSTON BAKED BEANS 25

CHIPOTLE CRUSTED PORK TENDERLOIN	26
PANCAKES	26
POLLO FAJITAS	27
BEEF AND BEAN CHIMICHANGAS	28
JUICIEST HAMBURGERS EVER	29
GARLIC GREEN BEANS	29
SUKI'S SPINACH AND FETA PASTA	30
TOFU PARMIGIANA	30
SIMPLE ROASTED BUTTERNUT SQUASH	31
KETTLE CORN	31
OVEN-FRIED PORK CHOPS	32
SIMPLE HAMBURGER STROGANOFF	32
SPICY VEGAN POTATO CURRY	33
EASY HONEY MUSTARD MOZZARELLA CHICKEN	34
QUINOA BLACK BEAN BURGERS	34
BROCCOLI BEEF	35
PENNE PASTA WITH SPINACH AND BACON	36
MEXICAN CASSEROLE	36
BEEF ENCHILADAS	37
EASY FRENCH DIP SANDWICHES	38
ZUCCHINI HERB CASSEROLE	38
BUTTERY COOKED CARROTS	39
PHILLY CHEESESTEAK SANDWICH WITH GARLIC MAYO	39
SIRLOIN STEAK WITH GARLIC BUTTER	40
MEXICAN BAKED FISH	41
INDIAN CHICKEN CURRY (MURGH KARI)	41
HEAVENLY HALIBUT	42
SARAH'S RICE PILAF	43
MONGOLIAN BEEF AND SPRING ONIONS	44
PARTY PINWHEELS	44
CHICKEN ASPARAGUS ROLL-UPS	45
PERFECT TEN BAKED COD	46
OLD-FASHIONED PANCAKES	47
BROCCOLI, RICE, CHEESE, AND CHICKEN CASSEROLE	47

Recipe	Page
SLIDER-STYLE MINI BURGERS	48
POTATO CHIPS	48
BEST GREEN BEAN CASSEROLE	49
AIMEE'S QUICK CHICKEN	50
EASY QUICHE	50
AWESOME HONEY PECAN PORK CHOPS	51
BEEF NACHO CASSEROLE	51
FAJITA SEASONING	52
GREEN BEANS WITH CHERRY TOMATOES	52
PERFECT MASHED POTATOES	53
EASY SAUSAGE GRAVY AND BISCUITS	53
FIERY FISH TACOS WITH CRUNCHY CORN SALSA	54
EGG AND SAUSAGE CASSEROLE	55
FRIED CABBAGE	55
CHINESE PEPPER STEAK	56
ONE PAN ORECCHIETTE PASTA	57
CHRIS' BAY AREA BURGER	57
SALSA CHICKEN BURRITO FILLING	58
GARLIC CHICKEN WITH ORZO NOODLES	58
CREAMY HERBED PORK CHOPS	59
SWEET AND SOUR SAUCE	60
SIMPLE BEEF STROGANOFF	60
SWEET AND SPICY GREEN BEANS	61
PORTOBELLO PENNE PASTA CASSEROLE	61
CANDIED CARROTS	62
BAKED CHICKEN WINGS	63
EASY CARAMELIZED ONION PORK CHOPS	63
TATER TOT TACO CASSEROLE	64
BACON FOR THE FAMILY OR A CROWD	65
KIELBASA AND CABBAGE	65
CAMPBELL'S GREEN BEAN CASSEROLE	66
BARBECUE BEEF CUPS	66
GARLIC MASHED CAULIFLOWER	67
UGLIES	67

LIME CILANTRO RICE	68
ANDREA'S PASTA FAGIOLI	68
QUICK BAKED ZUCCHINI CHIPS	69
RANCH BURGERS	70
DIJON-TARRAGON CREAM CHICKEN	70
SPICY CHIPOTLE TURKEY BURGERS	71
CHICKEN AND CORN CHILI	71
OVEN FRESH SEASONED POTATO WEDGES	72
CANDIED YAMS	72
THE BEST SWEET AND SOUR MEATBALLS	73
ASPARAGUS PARMESAN	74
SEARED AHI TUNA STEAKS	74
BEER BATTER FISH MADE GREAT	75
CARROT RICE	75
PIZZA PINWHEELS	76
GREEK PENNE AND CHICKEN	77
FRESH TOMATO SALSA	77
JAY'S JERK CHICKEN	78
COCONUT CURRY TOFU	79
PORK CHOPS WITH FRESH TOMATO, ONION, GARLIC, AND FETA	79
FETA CHICKEN	80
ASIAN COCONUT RICE	81
BAKED COCONUT SHRIMP	81
BREAKFAST PIES	82
SALMON PATTIES	82
CHICKEN BREASTS WITH LIME SAUCE	83
SIMPLE MACARONI AND CHEESE	83
CREAMED CHIPPED BEEF ON TOAST	84
GRILLED SAUSAGE WITH POTATOES AND GREEN BEANS	85
KIELBASA WITH PEPPERS AND POTATOES	85
GREEN BEAN AND MUSHROOM MEDLEY	86
SMOKY GRILLED PORK CHOPS	86
CHILI DOG CASSEROLE	87
BEST TUNA MELT (NEW JERSEY DINER STYLE)	88

GINGER VEGGIE STIR-FRY	88
CHICKEN FIESTA SALAD	89
SPICY CHICKEN BREASTS	90
CHICKEN BREASTS WITH HERB BASTING SAUCE	90
QUICK BRUSCHETTA CHICKEN BAKE	91

BAKED ASPARAGUS WITH BALSAMIC BUTTER SAUCE

Servings: 4 | Prep: 10m | Cooks: 12m | Total: 25m | Additional: 3m

NUTRITION FACTS

Calories: 77 | Carbohydrates: 4.9g | Fat: 5.9g | Protein: 2.8g | Cholesterol: 15mg

INGREDIENTS

- 1 pound fresh asparagus, trimmed
- 2 tablespoons butter
- cooking spray
- 1 tablespoon soy sauce
- salt and pepper to taste
- 1 teaspoon balsamic vinegar

DIRECTIONS

1. Preheat oven to 400 degrees F (200 degrees C).
2. Arrange the asparagus on a baking sheet. Coat with cooking spray, and season with salt and pepper.
3. Bake asparagus 12 minutes in the preheated oven, or until tender.
4. Melt the butter in a saucepan over medium heat. Remove from heat, and stir in soy sauce and balsamic vinegar. Pour over the baked asparagus to serve.

EASY MEXICAN CASSEROLE

Servings: 6 | Prep: 20m | Cooks: 30m | Total: 50m

NUTRITION FACTS

Calories: 632 | Carbohydrates: 32.8g | Fat: 43.7g | Protein: 31.7g | Cholesterol: 119mg

INGREDIENTS

- 1 pound lean ground beef
- 1 (2 ounce) can sliced black olives, drained
- 2 cups salsa
- 1/2 cup chopped green onion
- 1 (16 ounce) can chili beans, drained
- 1/2 cup chopped fresh tomato
- 3 cups tortilla chips, crushed
- 2 cups shredded Cheddar cheese
- 2 cups sour cream

DIRECTIONS

1. Preheat oven to 350 degrees F (175 degrees C).
2. In a large skillet over medium-high heat, cook ground beef until no longer pink. Stir in salsa, reduce heat, and simmer 20 minutes, or until liquid is absorbed. Stir in beans, and heat through.
3. Spray a 9x13 baking dish with cooking spray. Spread crushed tortilla chips in dish, and then spoon beef mixture over chips. Spread sour cream over beef, and sprinkle olives, green onion, and tomato over the sour cream. Top with Cheddar cheese.
4. Bake in preheated oven for 30 minutes, or until hot and bubbly.

ITALIAN BREADED PORK CHOPS

Servings: 4 | Prep: 25m | Cooks: 35m | Total: 1h

NUTRITION FACTS

Calories: 440 | Carbohydrates: 33.4g | Fat: 20.3g | Protein: 30g | Cholesterol: 186mg

INGREDIENTS

- 3 eggs, lightly beaten
- 2 tablespoons dried parsley
- 3 tablespoons milk
- 2 tablespoons olive oil
- 1 1/2 cups Italian seasoned bread crumbs
- 4 cloves garlic, peeled and chopped
- 1/2 cup grated Parmesan cheese
- 4 pork chops

DIRECTIONS

1. Preheat oven to 325 degrees F (160 degrees C).
2. In a small bowl, beat together the eggs and milk. In a separate small bowl, mix the bread crumbs, Parmesan cheese, and parsley.
3. Heat the olive oil in a large, oven-proof skillet over medium heat. Stir in the garlic, and cook until lightly browned. Remove garlic, reserving for other uses.
4. Dip each pork chop into the egg mixture, then into the bread crumb mixture, coating evenly. Place coated pork chops in the skillet, and brown abut 5 minutes on each side.
5. Place the skillet and pork chops in the preheated oven, and cook 25 minutes, or to an internal temperature of 145 degrees F (63 degrees C).

UNBELIEVABLE CHICKEN

Servings: 6 | Prep: 15m | Cooks: 20m | Total: 9h | Additional: 8h25m

NUTRITION FACTS

Calories: 337.1 | Carbohydrates: 22.4g | Protein: 24.8g | Cholesterol: 67.1mg

INGREDIENTS

- 1/4 cup cider vinegar
- 1/2 cup brown sugar
- 3 tablespoons prepared coarse-ground mustard
- 1 1/2 teaspoons salt
- 3 cloves garlic, peeled and minced
- 1 teaspoon ground black pepper to taste
- 1 lime, juiced
- 6 tablespoons olive oil
- 1/2 lemon, juiced
- 6 skinless, boneless chicken breast halves

DIRECTIONS

1. In a large glass bowl, mix the cider vinegar, mustard, garlic, lime juice, lemon juice, brown sugar, salt, and pepper. Whisk in the olive oil. Place chicken in the mixture. Cover, and marinate 8 hours, or overnight.
2. Preheat an outdoor grill for high heat.
3. Lightly oil the grill grate. Place chicken on the prepared grill, and cook 6 to 8 minutes per side, until juices run clear. Discard marinade.

LEMON GARLIC TILAPIA

Servings: 4 | Prep: 10m | Cooks: 30m | Total: 40m

NUTRITION FACTS

Calories: 142 | Carbohydrates: 1.4g | Fat: 4.4g | Protein: 23.1g | Cholesterol: 49mg

INGREDIENTS

- 4 tilapia fillets
- 1 clove garlic, finely chopped
- 3 tablespoons fresh lemon juice
- 1 teaspoon dried parsley flakes
- 1 tablespoon butter, melted
- pepper to taste

DIRECTIONS

1. Preheat oven to 375 degrees F (190 degrees C). Spray a baking dish with non-stick cooking spray.
2. Rinse tilapia fillets under cool water, and pat dry with paper towels.

3. Place fillets in baking dish. Pour lemon juice over fillets, then drizzle butter on top. Sprinkle with garlic, parsley, and pepper.
4. Bake in preheated oven until the fish is white and flakes when pulled apart with a fork, about 30 minutes.

HUMMUS
Servings: 16 | Prep: 10m | Cooks: 10m | Total: 16m

NUTRITION FACTS

Calories: 77 | Carbohydrates: 8.1g | Fat: 4.3g | Protein: 2.6g | Cholesterol: 0mg

INGREDIENTS

- 2 cups canned garbanzo beans, drained
- 2 cloves garlic, halved
- 1/3 cup tahini
- 1 tablespoon olive oil
- 1/4 cup lemon juice
- 1 pinch paprika
- 1 teaspoon salt
- 1 teaspoon minced fresh parsley

DIRECTIONS

1. Place the garbanzo beans, tahini, lemon juice, salt and garlic in a blender or food processor. Blend until smooth. Transfer mixture to a serving bowl.
2. Drizzle olive oil over the garbanzo bean mixture. Sprinkle with paprika and parsley.

CREAM CORN LIKE NO OTHER
Servings: 8 | Prep: 5m | Cooks: 10m | Total: 15m

NUTRITION FACTS

Calories: 253 | Carbohydrates: 24.8g | Fat: 16.5g | Protein: 5.1g | Cholesterol: 54mg

INGREDIENTS

- 2 (10 ounce) packages frozen corn kernels, thawed
- 2 tablespoons butter
- 1 cup heavy cream
- 1 cup whole milk
- 1 teaspoon salt
- 2 tablespoons all-purpose flour

- 2 tablespoons granulated sugar
- 1/4 cup freshly grated Parmesan cheese
- 1/4 teaspoon freshly ground black pepper

DIRECTIONS

1. In a skillet over medium heat, combine the corn, cream, salt, sugar, pepper and butter. Whisk together the milk and flour, and stir into the corn mixture. Cook stirring over medium heat until the mixture is thickened, and corn is cooked through. Remove from heat, and stir in the Parmesan cheese until melted. Serve hot.

ORZO WITH PARMESAN AND BASIL

Servings: 4 | Prep: 10m | Cooks: 20m | Total: 30m

NUTRITION FACTS

Calories: 299 | Carbohydrates: 42.2g | Fat: 9.4g | Protein: 11.6g | Cholesterol: 24mg

INGREDIENTS

- 2 tablespoons butter
- 1/4 cup chopped fresh basil
- 1 cup uncooked orzo pasta
- salt and pepper to taste
- 1 (14.5 ounce) can chicken broth
- 2 tablespoons chopped fresh basil
- 1/2 cup grated Parmesan cheese

DIRECTIONS

1. Melt butter in heavy skillet over medium-high heat. Stir in orzo and saute until lightly browned.
2. Stir in chicken stock and bring to boil. Cover. Reduce heat and simmer until orzo is tender and liquid is absorbed, about 15 - 20 minutes.
3. Mix in Parmesan cheese and basil. Season with salt and pepper. Transfer to shallow bowl. Garnish with basil sprigs.

SPAGHETTI CARBONARA

Servings: 8 | Prep: 20m | Cooks: 20m | Total: 40m

NUTRITION FACTS

Calories: 444 | Carbohydrates: 44.7g | Fat: 21.1g | Protein: 16.4g | Cholesterol: 118mg

INGREDIENTS

- 1 pound spaghetti
- 1/4 cup dry white wine (optional)
- 1 tablespoon olive oil
- 4 eggs
- 8 slices bacon, diced
- 1/2 cup grated Parmesan cheese
- 1 tablespoon olive oil
- 1 pinch salt and black pepper to taste
- 1 onion, chopped
- 2 tablespoons chopped fresh parsley
- 1 clove garlic, minced
- 2 tablespoons grated Parmesan cheese

DIRECTIONS

1. In a large pot of boiling salted water, cook spaghetti pasta until al dente. Drain well. Toss with 1 tablespoon of olive oil, and set aside.
2. Meanwhile in a large skillet, cook chopped bacon until slightly crisp; remove and drain onto paper towels. Reserve 2 tablespoons of bacon fat; add remaining 1 tablespoon olive oil, and heat in reused large skillet. Add chopped onion, and cook over medium heat until onion is translucent. Add minced garlic, and cook 1 minute more. Add wine if desired; cook one more minute.
3. Return cooked bacon to pan; add cooked and drained spaghetti. Toss to coat and heat through, adding more olive oil if it seems dry or is sticking together. Add beaten eggs and cook, tossing constantly with tongs or large fork until eggs are barely set. Quickly add 1/2 cup Parmesan cheese, and toss again. Add salt and pepper to taste (remember that bacon and Parmesan are very salty).
4. Serve immediately with chopped parsley sprinkled on top, and extra Parmesan cheese at table.

TACO PIE

Servings: 8 | Prep: 20m | Cooks: 10m | Total: 30m

NUTRITION FACTS

Calories: 687 | Carbohydrates: 50.6g | Fat: 43.4g | Protein: 24.4g | Cholesterol: 100mg

INGREDIENTS

- 1 (8 ounce) package refrigerated crescent rolls
- 1 (16 ounce) container sour cream
- 1 pound ground beef
- 8 ounces shredded Mexican-style cheese blend
- 1 (1 ounce) package taco seasoning mix
- 1 (14 ounce) bag tortilla chips, crushed

DIRECTIONS

1. Preheat oven to 350 degrees F (175 degrees C).
2. Lay crescent dough flat on the bottom of a square cake pan and bake according to package directions.
3. Meanwhile, brown the ground beef in a large skillet over medium high heat. Add the taco seasoning and stir together well. When dough is done, remove from oven and place meat mixture on top, then layer with sour cream and cheese, and then top off with the crushed nacho chips.
4. Return to oven and bake at 350 degrees F (175 degrees C) for 10 minutes, or until cheese has melted.

APPLE STRUDEL MUFFINS

Servings: 12 | Prep: 20m | Cooks: 20m | Total: 1h | Additional: 20m

NUTRITION FACTS

Calories: 264 | Carbohydrates: 41.4g | Fat: 9.7g | Protein: 3.4g | Cholesterol: 54mg

INGREDIENTS

- 2 cups all-purpose flour
- 1 1/4 teaspoons vanilla
- 1 teaspoon baking powder
- 1 1/2 cups chopped apples
- 1/2 teaspoon baking soda
- 1/3 cup packed brown sugar
- 1/2 teaspoon salt
- 1 tablespoon all-purpose flour
- 1/2 cup butter
- 1/8 teaspoon ground cinnamon
- 1 cup white sugar
- 1 tablespoon butter
- 2 eggs

DIRECTIONS

1. Preheat oven to 375 degrees F (190 degrees C). Grease a 12 cup muffin pan.
2. In a medium bowl, mix flour, baking powder, baking soda and salt.
3. In a large bowl, beat together butter, sugar and eggs until smooth. Mix in vanilla. Stir in apples, and gradually blend in the flour mixture. Spoon the mixture into the prepared muffin pan.
4. In a small bowl, mix brown sugar, flour and cinnamon. Cut in butter until mixture is like coarse crumbs. Sprinkle over tops of mixture in muffin pan.
5. Bake 20 minutes in the preheated oven, or until a toothpick inserted in the center of a muffin comes out clean. Allow to sit 5 minutes before removing muffins from pan. Cool on a wire rack.

SPANISH RICE

Servings: 4 | Prep: 10m | Cooks: 30m | Total: 40m

NUTRITION FACTS

Calories: 270 | Carbohydrates: 45.7g | Fat: 7.6g | Protein: 4.8g | Cholesterol: 0mg

INGREDIENTS

- 2 tablespoons vegetable oil
- 2 cups water
- 1 cup uncooked white rice
- 1 (10 ounce) can diced tomatoes and green chiles
- 1 onion, chopped
- 2 teaspoons chili powder, or to taste
- 1/2 green bell pepper, chopped
- 1 teaspoon salt

DIRECTIONS

1. Heat oil in a deep skillet over medium heat. Saute rice, onion, and bell pepper until rice is browned and onions are tender.
2. Stir in water and tomatoes. Season with chili powder and salt. Cover, and simmer for 30 minutes, or until rice is cooked and liquid is absorbed.

BAKED CHICKEN NUGGETS

Servings: 6 | Prep: 20m | Cooks: 20m | Total: 40m

NUTRITION FACTS

Calories: 308.4 | Carbohydrates: 14.6g | Protein: 19.3g | Cholesterol: 81mg

INGREDIENTS

- 3 skinless, boneless chicken breasts
- 1 teaspoon dried thyme
- 1 cup Italian seasoned bread crumbs
- 1 tablespoon dried basil
- 1/2 cup grated Parmesan cheese
- 1/2 cup butter, melted
- 1 teaspoon salt

DIRECTIONS

1. Preheat oven to 400 degrees F (200 degrees C).
2. Cut chicken breasts into 1 1/2-inch sized pieces. In a medium bowl, mix together the bread crumbs, cheese, salt, thyme and basil. Mix well. Put melted butter in a bowl or dish for dipping.
3. Dip chicken pieces into the melted butter first, then coat with the breadcrumb mixture. Place the well-coated chicken pieces on a lightly greased cookie sheet in a single layer, and bake in the preheated oven for 20 minutes.

SAUTEED APPLES

Servings: 8 | Prep: 5m | Cooks: 15m | Total: 20m

NUTRITION FACTS

Calories: 143 | Carbohydrates: 24.3g | Fat: 5.9g | Protein: 0.4g | Cholesterol: 15mg

INGREDIENTS

- 1/4 cup butter
- 1/2 cup cold water
- 4 large tart apples - peeled, cored and sliced 1/4 inch thick
- 1/2cup brown sugar
- 2 teaspoons cornstarch
- 1/2teaspoon ground cinnamon

DIRECTIONS

1. In a large skillet or saucepan, melt butter over medium heat; add apples. Cook, stirring constantly, until apples are almost tender, about 6 to 7 minutes.
2. Dissolve cornstarch in water; add to skillet. Stir in brown sugar and cinnamon. Boil for 2 minutes, stirring occasionally. Remove from heat and serve warm.

A GOOD EASY GARLIC CHICKEN

Servings: 4 | Prep: 10m | Cooks: 10m | Total: 20m

NUTRITION FACTS

Calories: 213.8 | Carbohydrates: 1.7g | Protein: 27.6g | Cholesterol: 91.3mg

INGREDIENTS

- 3 tablespoons butter
- 1 teaspoon seasoning salt
- 4 skinless, boneless chicken breast halves
- 1 teaspoon onion powder
- 2 teaspoons garlic powder

DIRECTIONS

1. Melt butter in a large skillet over medium high heat. Add chicken and sprinkle with garlic powder, seasoning salt and onion powder. Saute about 10 to 15 minutes on each side, or until chicken is cooked through and juices run clear.

EASY TUNA CASSEROLE

Servings: 8 | Prep: 15m | Cooks: 30m | Total: 45m

NUTRITION FACTS

Calories: 462 | Carbohydrates: 37.1g | Fat: 28.5g | Protein: 11.5g | Cholesterol: 23mg

INGREDIENTS

- 3 cups cooked macaroni
- 1 cup shredded Cheddar cheese
- 1 (5 ounce) can tuna, drained
- 1 1/2 cups French fried onions
- 1 (10.75 ounce) can condensed cream of chicken soup

DIRECTIONS

1. Preheat oven to 350 degrees F (175 degrees C).
2. In a 9x13-inch baking dish, combine the macaroni, tuna, and soup. Mix well, and then top with cheese.
3. Bake at 350 degrees F (175 degrees C) for about 25 minutes, or until bubbly. Sprinkle with fried onions, and bake for another 5 minutes. Serve hot.

FRENCH TOAST CASSEROLE

Servings: 6 | Prep: 30m | Cooks: 50m | Total: 1h20m

NUTRITION FACTS

Calories: 207 | Carbohydrates: 26.6g | Fat: 7.2g | Protein: 8.5g | Cholesterol: 129mg

INGREDIENTS

- 5 cups bread cubes
- 1/4 teaspoon salt
- 4 eggs
- 1 teaspoon vanilla extract
- 1 1/2 cups milk
- 1 tablespoon margarine, softened

- 1/4 cup white sugar, divided
- 1 teaspoon ground cinnamon

DIRECTIONS

1. Preheat oven to 350 degrees F (175 degrees C). Lightly butter an 8x8 inch baking pan.
2. Line bottom of pan with bread cubes. In a large bowl, beat together eggs, milk, 2 tablespoons sugar, salt and vanilla. pour egg mixture over bread. Dot with margarine; let stand for 10 minutes.
3. Combine remaining 2 tablespoons sugar with 1 teaspoon cinnamon and sprinkle over the top. Bake in preheated oven about 45 to 50 minutes, until top is golden.

SOUR CREAM PORK CHOPS

Servings: 6 | Prep: 15m | Cooks: 8h30m | Total: 8h45m

NUTRITION FACTS

Calories: 257 | Carbohydrates: 14.3g | Fat: 14.4g | Protein: 16.8g | Cholesterol: 54mg

INGREDIENTS

- 6 pork chops
- 2 cubes chicken bouillon
- salt and pepper to taste
- 2 cups boiling water
- garlic powder to taste
- 2 tablespoons all-purpose flour
- 1/2 cup all-purpose flour
- 1 (8 ounce) container sour cream
- 1 large onion, sliced 1/4 inch thick

DIRECTIONS

1. Season pork chops with salt, pepper, and garlic powder, and then dredge in 1/2 cup flour. In a skillet over medium heat, lightly brown chops in a small amount of oil.
2. Place chops in slow cooker, and top with onion slices. Dissolve bouillon cubes in boiling water and pour over chops. Cover, and cook on Low 7 to 8 hours.
3. Preheat oven to 200 degrees F (95 degrees C).
4. After the chops have cooked, transfer chops to the oven to keep warm. Be careful, the chops are so tender they will fall apart. In a small bowl, blend 2 tablespoons flour with the sour cream; mix into meat juices. Turn slow cooker to High for 15 to 30 minutes, or until sauce is slightly thickened. Serve sauce over pork chops.

SLOW COOKER LEMON GARLIC CHICKEN

Servings: 6 | Prep: 15m | Cooks: 3h15m | Total: 3h30m

NUTRITION FACTS

Calories: 192.3 | Carbohydrates: 1.3g | Protein: 29.6g | Cholesterol: 88.2mg

INGREDIENTS

- 1 teaspoon dried oregano
- 1/4 cup water
- 1/2 teaspoon salt
- 3 tablespoons fresh lemon juice
- 1/4 teaspoon ground black pepper
- 2 cloves garlic, minced
- 2 pounds skinless, boneless chicken breast halves
- 1 teaspoon chicken bouillon granules
- 2 tablespoons butter
- 1 teaspoon chopped fresh parsley

DIRECTIONS

1. In a bowl, mix the oregano, salt, and pepper. Rub the mixture into chicken. Melt the butter in a skillet over medium heat. Brown chicken in butter for 3 to 5 minutes on each side. Place chicken in a slow cooker.
2. In the same skillet, mix the water, lemon juice, garlic, and bouillon. Bring the mixture to boil. Pour over the chicken in the slow cooker.
3. Cover, and cook on High for 3 hours, or Low for 6 hours. Add the parsley to the slow cooker 15 to 30 minutes before the end of the cook time.

GREEK CHICKEN PASTA

Servings: 6 | Prep: 15m | Cooks: 15m | Total: 30m

NUTRITION FACTS

Calories: 487.7 | Carbohydrates: 70g | Protein: 32.6g | Cholesterol: 55mg

INGREDIENTS

- 1 (16 ounce) package linguine pasta
- 1/2 cup crumbled feta cheese
- 1/2 cup chopped red onion
- 3 tablespoons chopped fresh parsley
- 1 tablespoon olive oil

- 2 tablespoons lemon juice
- 2 cloves garlic, crushed
- 2 teaspoons dried oregano
- 1 pound skinless, boneless chicken breast meat - cut into bite-size pieces
- salt and pepper to taste
- 1 (14 ounce) can marinated artichoke hearts, drained and chopped
- 2 lemons, wedged, for garnish
- 1 large tomato, chopped

DIRECTIONS

1. Bring a large pot of lightly salted water to a boil. Cook pasta in boiling water until tender yet firm to the bit, 8 to 10 minutes; drain.
2. Heat olive oil in a large skillet over medium-high heat. Add onion and garlic; saute until fragrant, about 2 minutes. Stir in the chicken and cook, stirring occasionally, until chicken is no longer pink in the center and the juices run clear, about 5 to 6 minutes.
3. Reduce heat to medium-low; add artichoke hearts, tomato, feta cheese, parsley, lemon juice, oregano, and cooked pasta. Cook and stir until heated through, about 2 to 3 minutes. Remove from heat, season with salt and pepper, and garnish with lemon wedges.

VEGETARIAN CHICKPEA SANDWICH FILLING

Servings: 3 | Prep: 20m | Cooks: 0m | Total: 20m

NUTRITION FACTS

Calories: 259 | Carbohydrates: 43.5g | Fat: 5.8g | Protein: 9.3g | Cholesterol: 2mg

INGREDIENTS

- 1 (19 ounce) can garbanzo beans, drained and rinsed
- 1 tablespoon lemon juice
- 1 stalk celery, chopped
- 1 teaspoon dried dill weed
- 1/2 onion, chopped
- salt and pepper to taste
- 1 tablespoon mayonnaise

DIRECTIONS

1. Drain and rinse chickpeas. Pour chickpeas into a medium size mixing bowl and mash with a fork. Mix in celery, onion, mayonnaise (to taste), lemon juice, dill, salt and pepper to taste. Watch Now.

SPICY BEAN SALSA

Servings: 12 | Prep: 10m | Cooks: 8h | Total: 8h10m | Additional: 8h

NUTRITION FACTS

Calories: 155 | Carbohydrates: 20.4g | Fat: 6.4g | Protein: 5g | Cholesterol: 0mg

INGREDIENTS

- 1 (15 ounce) can black-eyed peas
- 1 (4 ounce) can diced jalapeno peppers
- 1 (15 ounce) can black beans, rinsed and drained
- 1 (14.5 ounce) can diced tomatoes, drained
- 1 (15 ounce) can whole kernel corn, drained
- 1 cup Italian-style salad dressing
- 1/2 cup chopped onion
- 1/2 teaspoon garlic salt
- 1/2 cup chopped green bell pepper

DIRECTIONS

1. In a medium bowl, combine black-eyed peas, black beans, corn, onion, green bell pepper, jalapeno peppers and tomatoes. Season with Italian-style salad dressing and garlic salt; mix well. Cover, and refrigerate overnight to blend flavors.

KEY WEST CHICKEN

Servings: 4 | Prep: 15m | Cooks: 15m | Total: 1h | Additional: 30m

NUTRITION FACTS

Calories: 184.1 | Carbohydrates: 5.6g | Protein: 25.3g | Cholesterol: 67.2mg

INGREDIENTS

- 3 tablespoons soy sauce
- 1 teaspoon lime juice
- 1 tablespoon honey
- 1 teaspoon chopped garlic
- 1 tablespoon vegetable oil
- 4 skinless, boneless chicken breast halves

DIRECTIONS

1. In a shallow container, blend soy sauce, honey, vegetable oil, lime juice, and garlic. Place chicken breast halves into the mixture, and turn to coat. Cover, and marinate in the refrigerator at least 30 minutes.
2. Preheat an outdoor grill for high heat.
3. Lightly oil the grill grate. Discard marinade, and grill chicken 6 to 8 minutes on each side, until juices run clear.

QUICK CHICKEN PICCATA

Servings: 4 | Prep: 10m | Cooks: 15m | Total: 25m

NUTRITION FACTS

Calories: 320.6 | Carbohydrates: 8.4g | Protein: 24.7g | Cholesterol: 87.5mg

INGREDIENTS

- 4 eaches skinless, boneless chicken breast halves
- 1/2 cup white wine
- 1 pinch cayenne pepper, or to taste
- 1/4 cup fresh lemon juice
- 1 pinch salt and ground black pepper to taste
- 1/4 cup water
- 1/4 cup all-purpose flour for dredging
- 3 tablespoons cold unsalted butter, cut in 1/4-inch slices
- 2 tablespoons olive oil
- 2 tablespoons fresh Italian parsley, chopped
- 1 tablespoon capers, drained

DIRECTIONS

1. Place chicken breasts between 2 layers of plastic wrap and pound to about 1/2-inch thick.
2. Season both sides of chicken breasts with cayenne, salt, and black pepper; dredge lightly in flour and shake off any excess.
3. Heat olive oil in a skillet over medium-high heat. Place chicken in the pan, reduce heat to medium, and cook until browned and cooked through, about 5 minutes per side; remove to a plate.
4. Cook capers in reserved oil, smashing them lightly to release brine, until warmed though, about 30 seconds.
5. Pour white wine into skillet. Scrape any browned bits from the bottom of the pan with a wooden spoon. Cook until reduced by half, about 2 minutes.
6. Stir lemon juice, water, and butter into the reduced wine mixture; cook and stir continuously to form a thick sauce, about 2 minutes. Reduce heat to low and stir parsley through the sauce.
7. Return chicken breasts to the pan cook until heated through, 1 to 2 minutes. Serve with sauce spooned over the top.

BANANA OAT MUFFINS

Servings: 12 | Prep: 15m | Cooks: 20m | Total: 35m

NUTRITION FACTS

Calories: 200 | Carbohydrates: 30.1g | Fat: 7.5g | Protein: 3.7g | Cholesterol: 17mg

INGREDIENTS

- 1 1/2 cups unbleached all-purpose flour
- 1 egg
- 1 cup rolled oats
- 3/4 cup milk
- 1/2 cup white sugar
- 1/3 cup vegetable oil
- 2 teaspoons baking powder
- 1/2 teaspoon vanilla extract
- 1 teaspoon baking soda
- 1 cup mashed bananas
- 1/2 teaspoon salt

DIRECTIONS

1. Combine flour, oats, sugar, baking powder, soda, and salt.
2. In a large bowl, beat the egg lightly. Stir in the milk, oil, and vanilla. Add the mashed banana, and combine thoroughly. Stir the flour mixture into the banana mixture until just combined. Line a 12-cup muffin tin with paper bake cups, and divide the batter among them.
3. Bake at 400 degrees F (205 degrees C) for 18 to 20 minutes.

AMAZING CHICKEN

Servings: 4 | Prep: 10m | Cooks: 30m | Total: 40m

NUTRITION FACTS

Calories: 547.8 | Carbohydrates: 40.9g | Protein: 32.8g | Cholesterol: 77.6mg

INGREDIENTS

- 4 skinless, boneless chicken breast halves
- 1 pinch salt and pepper to taste
- 1/2 cup mayonnaise
- 2 cups Italian seasoned bread crumbs

DIRECTIONS

1. Preheat the oven to 425 degrees F (220 degrees C). Grease a shallow baking dish.
2. Season chicken breasts. Coat chicken on all sides with mayonnaise, and roll in bread crumbs until coated. Place coated breasts into the prepared pan.
3. Bake uncovered for 30 minutes in the preheated oven, or until chicken is no longer pink in the middle and the juices run clear.

RED LENTIL CURRY

Servings: 12 | Prep: 10m | Cooks: 30m | Total: 40m

NUTRITION FACTS

Calories: 192 | Carbohydrates: 32.5g | Fat: 2.6g | Protein: 12.1g | Cholesterol: 0mg

INGREDIENTS

- 2 cups red lentils
- 1 teaspoon chili powder
- 1 large onion, diced
- 1 teaspoon salt
- 1 tablespoon vegetable oil
- 1 teaspoon white sugar
- 2 tablespoons curry paste
- 1 teaspoon minced garlic
- 1 tablespoon curry powder
- 1 teaspoon minced fresh ginger
- 1 teaspoon ground turmeric
- 1 (14.25 ounce) can tomato puree
- 1 teaspoon ground cumin

DIRECTIONS

1. Wash the lentils in cold water until the water runs clear. Put lentils in a pot with enough water to cover; bring to a boil, place a cover on the pot, reduce heat to medium-low, and simmer, adding water during cooking as needed to keep covered, until tender, 15 to 20 minutes. Drain.
2. Heat vegetable oil in a large skillet over medium heat; cook and stir onions in hot oil until caramelized, about 20 minutes.
3. Mix curry paste, curry powder, turmeric, cumin, chili powder, salt, sugar, garlic, and ginger together in a large bowl; stir into the onions. Increase heat to high and cook, stirring constantly, until fragrant, 1 to 2 minutes.
4. Stir in the tomato puree, remove from heat and stir into the lentils.

UNSTUFFED CABBAGE ROLL

Servings: 6 | Prep: 20m | Cooks: 35m | Total: 55m

NUTRITION FACTS

Calories: 398 | Carbohydrates: 16.3g | Fat: 23.8g | Protein: 28.5g | Cholesterol: 93mg

INGREDIENTS

- 2 pounds ground beef
- 1/2 cup water
- 1 large onion, chopped
- 2 cloves garlic, minced
- 1 small head cabbage, chopped
- 2 teaspoons salt
- 2 (14.5 ounce) cans diced tomatoes
- 1 teaspoon ground black pepper
- 1 (8 ounce) can tomato sauce

DIRECTIONS

1. Heat a Dutch oven or large skillet over medium-high heat. Cook and stir beef and onion in the hot Dutch oven until browned and crumbly, 5 to 7 minutes; drain and discard grease. Add cabbage, tomatoes, tomato sauce, water, garlic, salt, and pepper and bring to a boil. Cover Dutch oven, reduce heat, and simmer until cabbage is tender, about 30 minutes.

BEEF BARLEY VEGETABLE SOUP

Servings: 10 | Prep: 20m | Cooks: 5h30m | Total: 5h50m

NUTRITION FACTS

Calories: 321 | Carbohydrates: 22.4g | Fat: 17.3g | Protein: 20g | Cholesterol: 62mg

INGREDIENTS

- 1 (3 pound) beef chuck roast
- 4 cups water
- 1/2 cup barley
- 4 cubes beef bouillon cube
- 1 bay leaf
- 1 tablespoon white sugar
- 2 tablespoons oil
- 1/4 teaspoon ground black pepper
- 3 carrots, chopped
- 1 (28 ounce) can chopped stewed tomatoes
- 3 stalks celery, chopped
- salt to taste

- 1 onion, chopped
- ground black pepper to taste
- 1 (16 ounce) package frozen mixed vegetables

DIRECTIONS

1. In a slow cooker, cook chuck roast until very tender (usually 4 to 5 hours on High, but can vary with different slow cookers). Add barley and bay leaf during the last hour of cooking. Remove meat, and chop into bite-size pieces. Discard bay leaf. Set beef, broth, and barley aside.
2. Heat oil in a large stock pot over medium-high heat. Saute carrots, celery, onion, and frozen mixed vegetables until tender. Add water, beef bouillon cubes, sugar, 1/4 teaspoon pepper, chopped stewed tomatoes, and beef/barley mixture. Bring to boil, reduce heat, and simmer 10 to 20 minutes. Season with additional salt and pepper to taste.

ASIAN BEEF WITH SNOW PEAS

Servings: 4 | Prep: 5m | Cooks: 10m | Total: 15m

NUTRITION FACTS

Calories: 203 | Carbohydrates: 9.7g | Fat: 10g | Protein: 16g | Cholesterol: 39mg

INGREDIENTS

- 3 tablespoons soy sauce
- 1 tablespoon minced fresh ginger root
- 2 tablespoons rice wine
- 1 tablespoon minced garlic
- 1 tablespoon brown sugar
- 1 pound beef round steak, cut into thin strips
- 1/2 teaspoon cornstarch
- 8 ounces snow peas
- 1 tablespoon vegetable oil

DIRECTIONS

1. In a small bowl, combine the soy sauce, rice wine, brown sugar and cornstarch. Set aside.
2. Heat oil in a wok or skillet over medium high heat. Stir-fry ginger and garlic for 30 seconds. Add the steak and stir-fry for 2 minutes or until evenly browned. Add the snow peas and stir-fry for an additional 3 minutes. Add the soy sauce mixture, bring to a boil, stirring constantly. Lower heat and simmer until the sauce is thick and smooth. Serve immediately.

TENDER ITALIAN BAKED CHICKEN

Servings: 4 | Prep: 10m | Cooks: 20m | Total: 30m

NUTRITION FACTS

Calories: 55.9 | Carbohydrates: 17.1g | Protein: 31.8g | Cholesterol: 91.6mg

INGREDIENTS

- 3/4 cup mayonnaise
- 3/4 cup Italian seasoned bread crumbs
- 1/2 cup grated Parmesan cheese
- 4 skinless, boneless chicken breast halves
- 3/4 teaspoon garlic powder

DIRECTIONS

1. Preheat oven to 425 degrees F (220 degrees C).
2. In a bowl, mix the mayonnaise, Parmesan cheese, and garlic powder. Place bread crumbs in a separate bowl. Dip chicken into the mayonnaise mixture, then into the bread crumbs to coat. Arrange coated chicken on a baking sheet.
3. Bake 20 minutes in the preheated oven, or until chicken juices run clear and coating is golden brown.

BOSTON BAKED BEANS

Servings: 6 | Prep: 30m | Cooks: 4h | Total: 5h | Additional: 30m

NUTRITION FACTS

Calories: 382 | Carbohydrates: 63.1g | Fat: 6.3g | Protein: 20.7g | Cholesterol: 14mg

INGREDIENTS

- 2 cups navy beans
- 1/4 teaspoon ground black pepper
- 1/2 pound bacon
- 1/4 teaspoon dry mustard
- 1 onion, finely diced
- 1/2 cup ketchup
- 3 tablespoons molasses
- 1 tablespoon Worcestershire sauce
- 2 teaspoons salt
- 1/4 cup brown sugar

DIRECTIONS

1. Soak beans overnight in cold water. Simmer the beans in the same water until tender, approximately 1 to 2 hours. Drain and reserve the liquid.

2. Preheat oven to 325 degrees F (165 degrees C).
3. Arrange the beans in a 2 quart bean pot or casserole dish by placing a portion of the beans in the bottom of dish, and layering them with bacon and onion.
4. In a saucepan, combine molasses, salt, pepper, dry mustard, ketchup, Worcestershire sauce and brown sugar. Bring the mixture to a boil and pour over beans. Pour in just enough of the reserved bean water to cover the beans. Cover the dish with a lid or aluminum foil.
5. Bake for 3 to 4 hours in the preheated oven, until beans are tender. Remove the lid about halfway through cooking, and add more liquid if necessary to prevent the beans from getting too dry.

CHIPOTLE CRUSTED PORK TENDERLOIN

Servings: 6 | Prep: 15m | Cooks: 20m | Total: 35m

NUTRITION FACTS

Calories: 183 | Carbohydrates: 11.7g | Fat: 6.1g | Protein: 20.4g | Cholesterol: 62mg

INGREDIENTS

- 1 teaspoon onion powder
- 1 1/2 teaspoons salt
- 1 teaspoon garlic powder
- 4 tablespoons brown sugar
- 3 tablespoons chipotle chile powder
- 2 (3/4 pound) pork tenderloins

DIRECTIONS

1. Preheat grill for medium-high heat.
2. In a large resealable plastic bag, combine the onion powder, garlic powder, chipotle chile powder, salt, and brown sugar. Place tenderloins in bag and shake, coating meat evenly. Refrigerate for 10 to 15 minutes.
3. Lightly oil grill grate, and arrange meat on grate. Cook for 20 minutes, turning meat every 5 minutes. Remove from grill, let stand for 5 to 10 minutes before slicing.

PANCAKES

Servings: 3 | Prep: 5m | Cooks: 10m | Total: 20m

NUTRITION FACTS

Calories: 315 | Carbohydrates: 40.2g | Fat: 13g | Protein: 9.1g | Cholesterol: 69mg

INGREDIENTS

- 1 cup all-purpose flour

- 1/4 teaspoon salt
- 1 tablespoon white sugar
- 1 cup milk
- 1 teaspoon baking powder
- 1 egg
- 1/2 teaspoon baking soda
- 2 tablespoons vegetable oil

DIRECTIONS

1. Preheat a lightly oiled griddle over medium-high heat. Watch Now
2. Combine flour, sugar, baking powder, baking soda and salt. Make a well in the center. In a separate bowl, beat together egg, milk and oil. Pour milk mixture into flour mixture. Beat until smooth. Watch Now
3. Pour or scoop the batter onto the hot griddle, using approximately 1/4 cup for each pancake. Brown on both sides and serve hot. Watch Now.

POLLO FAJITAS

Servings: 5 | Prep: 15m | Cooks: 10m | Total: 55m | Additional: 30m

NUTRITION FACTS

Calories: 209.7 | Carbohydrates: 5.7g | Protein: 27.6g | Cholesterol: 113mg

INGREDIENTS

- 1 tablespoon Worcestershire sauce
- 1 1/2 pounds boneless, skinless chicken thighs, cut into strips
- 1 tablespoon cider vinegar
- 1 tablespoon vegetable oil
- 1 tablespoon soy sauce
- 1 onion, thinly sliced
- 1 teaspoon chili powder
- 1 green bell pepper, sliced
- 1 clove garlic, minced
- 1/2 lemon, juiced
- 1 dash hot pepper sauce

DIRECTIONS

1. In a medium bowl, combine Worcestershire sauce, vinegar, soy sauce, chili powder, garlic and hot pepper sauce. Place chicken in sauce, and turn once to coat. Marinate for 30 minutes at room temperature, or cover and refrigerate for several hours.

2. Heat oil in a large skillet over high heat. Add chicken strips to the pan, and saute for 5 minutes. Add the onion and green pepper, and saute another 3 minutes. Remove from heat, and sprinkle with lemon juice.

BEEF AND BEAN CHIMICHANGAS
Servings: 8 | Prep: 15m | Cooks: 30m | Total: 45m

NUTRITION FACTS

Calories: 821 | Carbohydrates: 83.6g | Fat: 36g | Protein: 40.1g | Cholesterol: 97mg

INGREDIENTS

- 1 pound lean ground beef
- 1 teaspoon ground cumin
- 3/4 cup chopped onion
- 1 (16 ounce) can refried beans
- 3/4 cup diced green bell pepper
- 8 (12 inch) flour tortillas
- 1 1/2 cups whole kernel corn
- 1 (16 ounce) package shredded Monterey Jack cheese
- 2 cups taco sauce
- 1 tablespoon butter, melted
- 2 teaspoons chili powder
- shredded lettuce
- 1 teaspoon garlic salt
- 1 tomato, diced

DIRECTIONS

1. Preheat the oven to 350 degrees F (175 degrees C).
2. Brown the ground beef in a skillet over medium-high heat. Drain excess grease, and add the onion, bell pepper, and corn. Cook for about 5 more minutes, or until vegetables are tender. Stir in the taco sauce, and season with chili powder, garlic salt and cumin, stirring until blended. Cook until heated through, then remove from heat, and set aside.
3. Open the can of beans, and spread a thin layer of beans onto each of the tortillas. Spoon the beef mixture down the center, and then top with as much shredded cheese as you like. Roll up the tortillas, and place them seam-side down onto a baking sheet. Brush the tortillas with melted butter.
4. Bake for 30 to 35 minutes in the preheated oven, or until golden brown. Serve with lettuce and tomato.

JUICIEST HAMBURGERS EVER

Servings: 8 | Prep: 15m | Cooks: 10m | Total: 35m | Additional: 10m

NUTRITION FACTS

Calories: 288 | Carbohydrates: 9.1g | Fat: 17.8g | Protein: 21.5g | Cholesterol: 96mg

INGREDIENTS

- 2 pounds ground beef
- 2 tablespoons Worcestershire sauce
- 1 egg, beaten
- 1/8 teaspoon cayenne pepper
- 3/4 cup dry bread crumbs
- 2 cloves garlic, minced
- 3 tablespoons evaporated milk

DIRECTIONS

1. Preheat grill for high heat.
2. In a large bowl, mix the ground beef, egg, bread crumbs, evaporated milk, Worcestershire sauce, cayenne pepper, and garlic using your hands. Form the mixture into 8 hamburger patties.
3. Lightly oil the grill grate. Grill patties 5 minutes per side, or until well done.

GARLIC GREEN BEANS

Servings: 5 | Prep: 10m | Cooks: 15m | Total: 25m

NUTRITION FACTS

Calories: 157 | Carbohydrates: 9.3g | Fat: 11.9g | Protein: 4g | Cholesterol: 11mg

INGREDIENTS

- 1 tablespoon butter
- 2 (14.5 ounce) cans green beans, drained
- 3 tablespoons olive oil
- salt and pepper to taste
- 1 medium head garlic - peeled and sliced
- 1/4 cup grated Parmesan cheese

DIRECTIONS

1. In a large skillet over medium heat, melt butter with olive oil; add garlic, and cook until lightly browned, stirring frequently. Stir in green beans, and season with salt and pepper. Cook until beans are tender, about 10 minutes. Remove from heat, and sprinkle with Parmesan cheese.

SUKI'S SPINACH AND FETA PASTA

Servings: 4 | Prep: 25m | Cooks: 15m | Total: 40m

NUTRITION FACTS

Calories: 451 | Carbohydrates: 51.8g | Fat: 20.6g | Protein: 17.5g | Cholesterol: 50mg

INGREDIENTS

- 1 (8 ounce) package penne pasta
- 1 cup sliced fresh mushrooms
- 2 tablespoons olive oil
- 2 cups spinach leaves, packed
- 1/2 cup chopped onion
- salt and pepper to taste
- 1 clove garlic, minced
- 1 pinch red pepper flakes
- 3 cups chopped tomatoes
- 8 ounces feta cheese, crumbled

DIRECTIONS

1. Bring a large pot of lightly salted water to a boil. Cook pasta in boiling water until al dente; drain.
2. Meanwhile, heat olive oil in a large skillet over medium-high heat; add onion and garlic, and cook until golden brown. Mix in tomatoes, mushrooms, and spinach. Season with salt, pepper, and red pepper flakes. Cook 2 minutes more, until tomatoes are heated through and spinach is wilted. Reduce heat to medium, stir in pasta and feta cheese, and cook until heated through.

TOFU PARMIGIANA

Servings: 4 | Prep: 25m | Cooks: 20m | Total: 45m

NUTRITION FACTS

Calories: 356.9 | Carbohydrates: 18.8g | Protein: 25.7g | Cholesterol: 23.8mg

INGREDIENTS

- 1/2 cup seasoned bread crumbs
- 2 tablespoons olive oil
- 5 tablespoons grated Parmesan cheese
- 1 (8 ounce) can tomato sauce
- 2 teaspoons dried oregano, divided
- 1/2 teaspoon dried basil
- salt to taste

- 1 clove garlic, minced
- ground black pepper to taste
- 4 ounces shredded mozzarella cheese
- 1 (12 ounce) package firm tofu

DIRECTIONS

1. In a small bowl, combine bread crumbs, 2 tablespoons Parmesan cheese, 1 teaspoon oregano, salt, and black pepper.
2. Slice tofu into 1/4 inch thick slices, and place in bowl of cold water. One at a time, press tofu slices into crumb mixture, turning to coat all sides.
3. Heat oil in a medium skillet over medium heat. Cook tofu slices until crisp on one side. Drizzle with a bit more olive oil, turn, and brown on the other side.
4. Combine tomato sauce, basil, garlic, and remaining oregano. Place a thin layer of sauce in an 8 inch square baking pan. Arrange tofu slices in the pan. Spoon remaining sauce over tofu. Top with shredded mozzarella and remaining 3 tablespoons Parmesan.
5. Bake at 400 degrees F (205 degrees C) for 20 minutes.

SIMPLE ROASTED BUTTERNUT SQUASH

Servings: 4 | Prep: 15m | Cooks: 25m | Total: 40m

NUTRITION FACTS

Calories: 177 | Carbohydrates: 30.3g | Fat: 7g | Protein: 2.6g | Cholesterol: 0mg

INGREDIENTS

- 1 butternut squash - peeled, seeded, and cut into 1-inch cubes
- 2 tablespoons olive oil
- 2 cloves garlic, minced
- salt and ground black pepper to taste

DIRECTIONS

1. Preheat oven to 400 degrees F (200 degrees C).
2. Toss butternut squash with olive oil and garlic in a large bowl. Season with salt and black pepper. Arrange coated squash on a baking sheet.
3. Roast in the preheated oven until squash is tender and lightly browned, 25 to 30 minutes.

KETTLE CORN

Servings: 5 | Prep: 5m | Cooks: 15m | Total: 20m

NUTRITION FACTS

Calories: 209 | Carbohydrates: 24.8g | Fat: 11.9g | Protein: 2.4g | Cholesterol: 0mg

INGREDIENTS

- 1/4 cup vegetable oil
- 1/4 cup white sugar
- 1/2 cup unpopped popcorn kernels

DIRECTIONS

1. Heat the vegetable oil in a large pot over medium heat. Once hot, stir in the sugar and popcorn. Cover, and shake the pot constantly to keep the sugar from burning. Once the popping has slowed to once every 2 to 3 seconds, remove the pot from the heat and continue to shake for a few minutes until the popping has stopped. Pour into a large bowl, and allow to cool, stirring occasionally to break up large clumps.

OVEN-FRIED PORK CHOPS

Servings: 4 | Prep: 10m | Cooks: 20m | Total: 30m

NUTRITION FACTS

Calories: 422 | Carbohydrates: 38.6g | Fat: 14.3g | Protein: 32.3g | Cholesterol: 128mg

INGREDIENTS

- 4 pork chops, trimmed
- 2 tablespoons milk
- 2 tablespoons butter, melted
- 1/4 teaspoon black pepper
- 1 egg, beaten
- 1 cup herb-seasoned dry bread stuffing mix

DIRECTIONS

1. Preheat oven to 425 degrees F (220 degrees C). Pour butter into a 9x13 inch baking pan.
2. Stir together egg, milk and pepper. Dip pork chops in egg mixture, coat with stuffing mix and place in pan.
3. Bake in preheated oven for 10 minutes. Turn chops and bake for another 10 minutes, or until no pink remains in the meat and juices run clear.

SIMPLE HAMBURGER STROGANOFF

Servings: 6 | Prep: 20m | Cooks: 10m | Total: 30m

NUTRITION FACTS

Calories: 735 | Carbohydrates: 60.9g | Fat: 42g | Protein: 28.9g | Cholesterol: 159mg

INGREDIENTS

- 1 (16 ounce) package egg noodles
- 1 (6 ounce) can chopped mushrooms, with liquid
- 1 pound lean ground beef
- 1/2 cup milk
- 1 (.75 ounce) packet dry brown gravy mix
- 1 (8 ounce) container sour cream
- 1 (8 ounce) package cream cheese
- 2 (10.75 ounce) cans condensed cream of mushroom soup

DIRECTIONS

1. Bring a large pot of lightly salted water to a boil. Add egg noodles and cook for 8 to 10 minutes or until al dente; drain.
2. In a skillet over medium heat, brown the ground beef until no pink shows, about 5 minutes; drain fat.
3. Mix brown gravy, cream cheese, and mushrooms with hamburger, stirring until cream cheese melts. Add milk, sour cream, and mushroom soup to cooked pasta. Blend hamburger mixture with pasta.

SPICY VEGAN POTATO CURRY

Servings: 6 | Prep: 30m | Cooks: 30m | Total: 1h

NUTRITION FACTS

Calories: 407 | Carbohydrates: 50.6g | Fat: 20.1g | Protein: 10.1g | Cholesterol: 0mg

INGREDIENTS

- 4 potatoes, peeled and cubed
- 4 teaspoons garam masala
- 2 tablespoons vegetable oil
- 1 (1 inch) piece fresh ginger root, peeled and minced
- 1 yellow onion, diced
- 2 teaspoons salt
- 3 cloves garlic, minced
- 1 (14.5 ounce) can diced tomatoes
- 2 teaspoons ground cumin
- 1 (15 ounce) can garbanzo beans (chickpeas), rinsed and drained
- 1 1/2 teaspoons cayenne pepper
- 1 (15 ounce) can peas, drained
- 4 teaspoons curry powder

- 1 (14 ounce) can coconut milk

DIRECTIONS

1. Place potatoes into a large pot and cover with salted water. Bring to a boil over high heat, then reduce heat to medium-low, cover, and simmer until just tender, about 15 minutes. Drain and allow to steam dry for a minute or two.
2. Meanwhile, heat the vegetable oil in a large skillet over medium heat. Stir in the onion and garlic; cook and stir until the onion has softened and turned translucent, about 5 minutes. Season with cumin, cayenne pepper, curry powder, garam masala, ginger, and salt; cook for 2 minutes more. Add the tomatoes, garbanzo beans, peas, and potatoes. Pour in the coconut milk, and bring to a simmer. Simmer 5 to 10 minutes before serving.

EASY HONEY MUSTARD MOZZARELLA CHICKEN

Servings: 4 | Prep: 15m | Cooks: 35m | Total: 50m

NUTRITION FACTS

Calories: 465.3 | Carbohydrates: 55g | Protein: 36.3g | Cholesterol: 95.1mg

INGREDIENTS

- 4 skinless, boneless chicken breast halves
- 1 pinch lemon pepper to taste
- 3/4 cup honey
- 4 slices bacon, cut in half
- 1/2 cup prepared mustard
- 1 cup shredded mozzarella cheese

DIRECTIONS

1. Preheat oven to 375 degrees F (190 degrees C).
2. Place the chicken breast halves in a baking dish, and drizzle evenly with honey and mustard. Sprinkle with lemon pepper.
3. Bake chicken 25 minutes in the preheated oven. Top each breast half with 2 bacon slice halves, and sprinkle evenly with cheese. Continue baking 10 minutes, or until chicken juices run clear, bacon is crisp, and cheese is bubbly.

QUINOA BLACK BEAN BURGERS

Servings: 5 | Prep: 15m | Cooks: 20m | Total: 35m

NUTRITION FACTS

Calories: 245 | Carbohydrates: 28.9g | Fat: 10.6g | Protein: 9.3g | Cholesterol: 37mg

INGREDIENTS

- 1 (15 ounce) can black beans, rinsed and drained
- 1 large clove garlic, minced
- 1/4 cup quinoa
- 1 1/2 teaspoons ground cumin
- 1/2 cup water
- 1/2 teaspoon salt
- 1/2 cup bread crumbs
- 1 teaspoon hot pepper sauce (such as Frank's RedHot)
- 1/4 cup minced yellow bell pepper
- 1 egg
- 2 tablespoons minced onion
- 3 tablespoons olive oil

DIRECTIONS

1. Bring the quinoa and water to a boil in a saucepan. Reduce heat to medium-low, cover, and simmer until the quinoa is tender and the water has been absorbed, about 15 to 20 minutes.
2. Roughly mash the black beans with a fork leaving some whole black beans in a paste-like mixture.
3. Mix the quinoa, bread crumbs, bell pepper, onion, garlic, cumin, salt, hot pepper sauce, and egg into the black beans using your hands.
4. Form the black bean mixture into 5 patties.
5. Heat the olive oil in a large skillet.
6. Cook the patties in the hot oil until heated through, 2 to 3 minutes per side.

BROCCOLI BEEF

Servings: 4 | Prep: 15m | Cooks: 15m | Total: 30m

NUTRITION FACTS

Calories: 178.4 | Carbohydrates: 19g | Protein: 19.2g | Cholesterol: 38.6mg

INGREDIENTS

- 1/4 cup all-purpose flour
- 1 pound boneless round steak, cut into bite size pieces
- 1 (10.5 ounce) can beef broth
- 1/4 teaspoon chopped fresh ginger root
- 2 tablespoons white sugar
- 1 clove garlic, minced
- 2 tablespoons soy sauce
- 4 cups chopped fresh broccoli

DIRECTIONS

1. In a small bowl, combine flour, broth, sugar, and soy sauce. Stir until sugar and flour are dissolved.
2. In a large skillet or wok over high heat, cook and stir beef 2 to 4 minutes, or until browned. Stir in broth mixture, ginger, garlic, and broccoli. Bring to a boil, then reduce heat. Simmer 5 to 10 minutes, or until sauce thickens.

PENNE PASTA WITH SPINACH AND BACON
Servings: 4 | Prep: 10m | Cooks: 15m | Total: 25m

NUTRITION FACTS

Calories: 517 | Carbohydrates: 73.8g | Fat: 14.8g | Protein: 21g | Cholesterol: 15mg

INGREDIENTS

- 1 (12 ounce) package penne pasta
- 2 tablespoons minced garlic
- 2 tablespoons olive oil, divided
- 1 (14.5 ounce) can diced tomatoes
- 6 slices bacon, chopped
- 1 bunch fresh spinach, rinsed and torn into bite-size pieces

DIRECTIONS

1. Bring a large pot of lightly salted water to a boil. Add the penne pasta, and cook until tender, 8 to 10 minutes.
2. Meanwhile, heat 1 tablespoon of olive oil in a skillet over medium heat. Place bacon in the skillet, and cook until browned and crisp. Add garlic, and cook for about 1 minute. Stir in the tomatoes, and cook until heated through.
3. Place the spinach into a colander, and drain the hot pasta over it so it is wilted. Transfer to a large serving bowl, and toss with the remaining olive oil, and the bacon and tomato mixture.

MEXICAN CASSEROLE
Servings: 5 | Prep: 15m | Cooks: 15m | Total: 30m

NUTRITION FACTS

Calories: 383.7 | Carbohydrates: 34g | Protein: 26.8g | Cholesterol: 59.1mg

INGREDIENTS

- 2 tablespoons vegetable oil
- 1/4 cup salsa

- 3/4 pound cubed skinless, boneless chicken breast meat
- water as needed
- 1/2 (1.25 ounce) package taco seasoning mix
- 1 cup shredded Mexican-style cheese
- 1 (15 ounce) can black beans, rinsed and drained
- 1 1/2 cups crushed plain tortilla chips
- 1 (8.75 ounce) can sweet corn, drained

DIRECTIONS

1. In a large skillet over medium high heat, saute chicken in oil until cooked through and no longer pink inside. Add taco seasoning, beans, corn, salsa and a little water to prevent drying out. Cover skillet and simmer over medium low heat for 10 minutes.
2. Preheat oven to 350 degrees F (175 degrees C).
3. Transfer chicken mixture to a 9x13 inch baking dish. Top with 1/2 cup of the cheese and crushed tortilla chips.
4. Bake in the preheated oven for 15 minutes. Add remaining 1/2 cup cheese and bake until cheese is melted and bubbly.

BEEF ENCHILADAS

Servings: 10 | Prep: 25m | Cooks: 20m | Total: 45m

NUTRITION FACTS

Calories: 448 | Carbohydrates: 40.5g | Fat: 21.1g | Protein: 22.2g | Cholesterol: 60mg

INGREDIENTS

- 1 pound lean ground beef
- 10 (10 inch) flour tortillas
- 1 small onion, chopped
- 2 cups shredded Cheddar cheese
- 1 (1.5 ounce) package dry enchilada sauce mix
- 1 (2.25 ounce) can sliced black olives, drained

DIRECTIONS

1. Preheat oven to 350 degrees F (175 degrees C). In a medium skillet over medium high heat, cook the ground beef and onion until beef is evenly browned and onion is tender.
2. Prepare the enchilada sauce according to package directions. Pour 1/4 cup of the sauce into the bottom of a 9x13 inch baking dish.
3. On each flour tortilla, place an equal portion of the ground beef mixture and about 1 ounce of Cheddar cheese, reserving at least 1/2 cup of cheese. Then tightly roll the tortillas and place seam side down in the baking dish.

4. Pour the remaining sauce over the top of the enchiladas and sprinkle with the remaining cheese and olives.
5. Bake in a preheated oven for 20 minutes, or until the sauce is bubbly and cheese is thoroughly melted.

EASY FRENCH DIP SANDWICHES
Servings: 4 | Prep: 5m | Cooks: 10m | Total: 15m

NUTRITION FACTS

Calories: 548 | Carbohydrates: 40.5g | Fat: 22.6g | Protein: 44.6g | Cholesterol: 94mg

INGREDIENTS

- 1 (10.5 ounce) can beef consomme
- 8 slices provolone cheese
- 1 cup water
- 4 hoagie rolls, split lengthwise
- 1 pound thinly sliced deli roast beef

DIRECTIONS

1. Preheat oven to 350 degrees F (175 degrees C). Open the hoagie rolls and lay out on a baking sheet.
2. Heat beef consomme and water in a medium saucepan over medium-high heat to make a rich beef broth. Place the roast beef in the broth and warm for 3 minutes. Arrange the meat on the hoagie rolls and top each roll with 2 slices of provolone.
3. Bake the sandwiches in the preheated oven for 5 minutes, or until the cheese just begins to melt. Serve the sandwiches with small bowls of the warm broth for dipping.

ZUCCHINI HERB CASSEROLE
Servings: 6 | Prep: 15m | Cooks: 40m | Total: 55m

NUTRITION FACTS

Calories: 266 | Carbohydrates: 16.5g | Fat: 17.5g | Protein: 12.4g | Cholesterol: 40mg

INGREDIENTS

- 1/3 cup uncooked long grain white rice
- 1 1/4 teaspoons garlic salt
- 2/3 cup water
- 1/2 teaspoon basil
- 2 tablespoons vegetable oil
- 1/2 teaspoon sweet paprika

- 1 1/2 pounds zucchini, cubed
- 1/2 teaspoon dried oregano
- 1 cup sliced green onions
- 1 1/2 cups seeded, chopped tomatoes
- 1 clove garlic, minced
- 2 cups shredded sharp Cheddar cheese, divided

DIRECTIONS

1. Combine the rice and water in a saucepan, and bring to a boil. Reduce heat to low, cover, and simmer 20 minutes, until rice is tender.
2. Preheat oven to 350 degrees F (175 degrees C). Lightly grease a shallow 1 1/2 quart casserole dish.
3. Heat the oil in a skillet over medium heat, and cook the zucchini, green onions, and garlic 5 minutes, or until tender. Season with garlic salt, basil, paprika, and oregano. Mix in the cooked rice, tomatoes, and 1 cup cheese. Continue to cook and stir until heated through. Transfer to the prepared casserole dish. Top with remaining cheese.
4. Bake uncovered 20 minutes, or until cheese is melted and bubbly.

BUTTERY COOKED CARROTS

Servings: 4 | Prep: 15m | Cooks: 10m | Total: 25m

NUTRITION FACTS

Calories: 185 | Carbohydrates: 21.2g | Fat: 11.4g | Protein: 0.9g | Cholesterol: 0mg

INGREDIENTS

- 1 pound baby carrots
- 1/4 cup margarine
- 1/3 cup brown sugar

DIRECTIONS

1. Cook carrots in a large pot of boiling water until tender. Drain off most of the liquid, leaving bottom of pan covered with water. Set the carrots aside.
2. Stir margarine and brown sugar into the water. Simmer and stir until the margarine melts. Return carrots to the pot, and toss to coat. Cover, and let sit for a few minutes to allow flavors to mingle.

PHILLY CHEESESTEAK SANDWICH WITH GARLIC MAYO

Servings: 4 | Prep: 10m | Cooks: 20m | Total: 30m

NUTRITION FACT

Calories: 935 | Carbohydrates: 49.6g | Fat: 66.4g | Protein: 35.3g | Cholesterol: 96mg

INGREDIENTS

- 1 cup mayonnaise
- 2 onions, sliced into rings
- 2 cloves garlic, minced
- salt and pepper to taste
- 1 tablespoon olive oil
- 4 hoagie rolls, split lengthwise and toasted
- 1 pound beef round steak, cut into thin strips
- 1 (8 ounce) package shredded mozzarella cheese
- 2 green bell peppers, cut into 1/4 inch strips
- 1 teaspoon dried oregano

DIRECTIONS

1. In a small bowl, combine mayonnaise and minced garlic. Cover, and refrigerate. Preheat oven to 500 degrees F (260 degrees C).
2. Heat oil in a large skillet over medium heat. Saute beef until lightly browned. Stir in green pepper and onion, and season with salt and pepper. Saute until vegetables are tender, and remove from heat.
3. Spread each bun generously with garlic mayonnaise. Divide beef mixture into the buns. Top with shredded cheese, and sprinkle with oregano. Place sandwiches on a baking pan.
4. Heat sandwiches in preheated oven, until cheese is melted or slightly browned.

SIRLOIN STEAK WITH GARLIC BUTTER

Servings: 8 | Prep: 20m | Cooks: 10m | Total: 30m

NUTRITION FACTS

Calories: 453 | Carbohydrates: 1g | Fat: 32.2g | Protein: 37.7g | Cholesterol: 151mg

INGREDIENTS

- 1/2 cup butter
- 4 pounds beef top sirloin steaks
- 2 teaspoons garlic powder
- salt and pepper to taste
- 4 cloves garlic, minced

DIRECTIONS

1. Preheat an outdoor grill for high heat.

2. In a small saucepan, melt butter over medium-low heat with garlic powder and minced garlic. Set aside.
3. Sprinkle both sides of each steak with salt and pepper.
4. Grill steaks 4 to 5 minutes per side, or to desired doneness. When done, transfer to warmed plates. Brush tops liberally with garlic butter, and allow to rest for 2 to 3 minutes before serving.

MEXICAN BAKED FISH

Servings: 6 | Prep: 15m | Cooks: 15m | Total: 30m

NUTRITION FACTS

Calories: 311 | Carbohydrates: 11.3g | Fat: 17.6g | Protein: 27.6g | Cholesterol: 69mg

INGREDIENTS

- 1 1/2 pounds cod
- 1/2 cup coarsely crushed corn chips
- 1 cup salsa
- 1 avocado - peeled, pitted and sliced
- 1 cup shredded sharp Cheddar cheese
- 1/4 cup sour cream

DIRECTIONS

1. Preheat oven to 400 degrees F (200 degrees C). Lightly grease one 8x12 inch baking dish.
2. Rinse fish fillets under cold water, and pat dry with paper towels. Lay fillets side by side in the prepared baking dish. Pour the salsa over the top, and sprinkle evenly with the shredded cheese. Top with the crushed corn chips.
3. Bake, uncovered, in the preheated oven for 15 minutes, or until fish is opaque and flakes with a fork. Serve topped with sliced avocado and sour cream.

INDIAN CHICKEN CURRY (MURGH KARI)

Servings: 6 | Prep: 20m | Cooks: 40m | Total: 1h

NUTRITION FACTS

Calories: 427.4 | Carbohydrates: 14.7g | Protein: 38.1g | Cholesterol: 94.7mg

INGREDIENTS

- 2 pounds skinless, boneless chicken breast halves
- 1 teaspoon cayenne pepper
- 2 teaspoons salt

- 1 tablespoon water
- 1/2 cup cooking oil
- 1 (15 ounce) can crushed tomatoes
- 1 1/2 cups chopped onion
- 1 cup plain yogurt
- 1 tablespoon minced garlic
- 1 tablespoon chopped fresh cilantro
- 1 1/2 teaspoons minced fresh ginger root
- 1 teaspoon salt
- 1 tablespoon curry powder
- 1/2 cup water
- 1 teaspoon ground cumin
- 1 teaspoon garam masala
- 1 teaspoon ground turmeric
- 1 tablespoon chopped fresh cilantro
- 1 teaspoon ground coriander
- 1 tablespoon fresh lemon juice

DIRECTIONS

1. Sprinkle the chicken breasts with 2 teaspoons salt.
2. Heat the oil in a large skillet over high heat; partially cook the chicken in the hot oil in batches until completely browned. Transfer the browned chicken breasts to a plate and set aside.
3. Reduce the heat under the skillet to medium-high; add the onion, garlic, and ginger to the oil remaining in the skillet and cook and stir until the onion turns translucent, about 8 minutes. Stir the curry powder, cumin, turmeric, coriander, cayenne, and 1 tablespoon of water into the onion mixture; allow to heat together for about 1 minute while stirring. Mix the tomatoes, yogurt, 1 tablespoon chopped cilantro, and 1 teaspoon salt into the mixture. Return the chicken breast to the skillet along with any juices on the plate. Pour 1/2 cup water into the mixture; bring to a boil, turning the chicken to coat with the sauce. Sprinkle the garam masala and 1 tablespoon cilantro over the chicken.
4. Cover the skillet and simmer until the chicken breasts are no longer pink in the center and the juices run clear, about 20 minutes. An instant-read thermometer inserted into the center should read at least 165 degrees F (74 degrees C). Sprinkle with lemon juice to serve.

HEAVENLY HALIBUT

Servings: 8 | Prep: 15m | Cooks: 10m | Total: 25m

NUTRITION FACTS

Calories: 235 | Carbohydrates: 0.9g | Fat: 13.9g | Protein: 25.7g | Cholesterol: 58mg

INGREDIENTS

- 1/2 cup grated Parmesan cheese
- 3 tablespoons chopped green onions
- 1/4 cup butter, softened
- 1/4 teaspoon salt
- 3 tablespoons mayonnaise
- 1 dash hot pepper sauce
- 2 tablespoons lemon juice
- 2 pounds skinless halibut fillets

DIRECTIONS

1. Preheat the oven broiler. Grease a baking dish.
2. In a bowl, mix the Parmesan cheese, butter, mayonnaise, lemon juice, green onions, salt, and hot pepper sauce.
3. Arrange the halibut fillets in the prepared baking dish.
4. Broil halibut fillets 8 minutes in the prepared oven, or until easily flaked with a fork. Spread with the Parmesan cheese mixture, and continue broiling 2 minutes, or until topping is bubbly and lightly browned.

SARAH'S RICE PILAF

Servings: 4 | Prep: 10m | Cooks: 35m | Total: 50m | Additional: 5m

NUTRITION FACTS

Calories: 244 | Carbohydrates: 40g | Fat: 6.5g | Protein: 5.9g | Cholesterol: 18mg

INGREDIENTS

- 2 tablespoons butter
- 2 cloves garlic, minced
- 1/2 cup orzo pasta
- 1/2 cup uncooked white rice
- 1/2 cup diced onion
- 2 cups chicken broth

DIRECTIONS

1. Melt the butter in a lidded skillet over medium-low heat. Cook and stir orzo pasta until golden brown. Stir in onion and cook until onion becomes translucent, then add garlic and cook for 1 minute. Mix in the rice and chicken broth. Increase heat to high and bring to a boil. Reduce heat to medium-low, cover, and simmer until the rice is tender, and the liquid has been absorbed, 20 to 25 minutes. Remove from heat and let stand for 5 minutes, then fluff with a fork.

MONGOLIAN BEEF AND SPRING ONIONS

Servings: 4 | Prep: 12m | Cooks: 8m | Total: 30m | Additional: 10m

NUTRITION FACTS

Calories: 391 | Carbohydrates: 54.7g | Fat: 12.1g | Protein: 18g | Cholesterol: 27mg

INGREDIENTS

- 2 teaspoons vegetable oil
- 2/3 cup dark brown sugar
- 1 tablespoon finely chopped garlic
- 1 pound beef flank steak, sliced 1/4 inch thick on the diagonal
- 1/2 teaspoon grated fresh ginger root
- 1/4 cup cornstarch
- 1/2 cup soy sauce
- 1 cup vegetable oil for frying
- 1/2 cup water
- 2 bunches green onions, cut in 2-inch lengths

DIRECTIONS

1. Heat 2 teaspoons of vegetable oil in a saucepan over medium heat, and cook and stir the garlic and ginger until they release their fragrance, about 30 seconds. Pour in the soy sauce, water, and brown sugar. Raise the heat to medium-high, and stir 4 minutes, until the sugar has dissolved and the sauce boils and slightly thickens. Remove sauce from the heat, and set aside.
2. Place the sliced beef into a bowl, and stir the cornstarch into the beef, coating it thoroughly. Allow the beef and cornstarch to sit until most of the juices from the meat have been absorbed by the cornstarch, about 10 minutes.
3. Heat the vegetable oil in a deep-sided skillet or wok to 375 degrees F (190 degrees C).
4. Shake excess cornstarch from the beef slices, and drop them into the hot oil, a few at a time. Stir briefly, and fry until the edges become crisp and start to brown, about 2 minutes. Remove the beef from the oil with a large slotted spoon, and allow to drain on paper towels to remove excess oil.
5. Pour the oil out of the skillet or wok, and return the pan to medium heat. Return the beef slices to the pan, stir briefly, and pour in the reserved sauce. Stir once or twice to combine, and add the green onions. Bring the mixture to a boil, and cook until the onions have softened and turned bright green, about 2 minutes.

PARTY PINWHEELS

Servings: 15 | Prep: 10m | Cooks: 5m | Total: 2h20m | Additional: 2h5m

NUTRITION FACTS

Calories: 229 | Carbohydrates: 18.6g | Fat: 14.5g | Protein: 5.9g | Cholesterol: 37mg

INGREDIENTS

- 2 (8 ounce) packages cream cheese, softened
- 1/2 cup red bell pepper, diced
- 1 (1 ounce) package ranch dressing mix
- 1/2 cup diced celery
- 2 green onions, minced
- 1 (2 ounce) can sliced black olives
- 4 (12 inch) flour tortillas
- 1/2 cup shredded Cheddar cheese

DIRECTIONS

1. In a medium-size mixing bowl, combine cream cheese, ranch dressing mix, and green onions. Spread this mixture on each tortilla. Sprinkle red pepper, celery, black olives, and cheese (if you'd like) over the cream cheese mixture. Roll up the tortillas, then wrap them tightly in aluminum foil.
2. Chill 2 hours or overnight. Cut off ends of the rolls, and slice the chilled rolls into 1 inch slices.

CHICKEN ASPARAGUS ROLL-UPS

Servings: 4 | Prep: 25m | Cooks: 30m | Total: 55m

NUTRITION FACTS

Calories: 530.2 | Carbohydrates: 28.8g | Protein: 36.8g | Cholesterol: 97.2mg

INGREDIENTS

- 1/2 cup mayonnaise
- 1/2 teaspoon salt
- 3 tablespoons Dijon mustard
- 16 spears fresh asparagus, trimmed
- 1 lemon, juiced and zested
- 4 skinless, boneless chicken breast halves
- 2 teaspoons dried tarragon
- 4 slices provolone cheese
- 1 teaspoon ground black pepper
- 1 cup panko bread crumbs

DIRECTIONS

1. Preheat oven to 475 degrees F (245 degrees C). Grease a baking dish. In a bowl, mix together the mayonnaise, Dijon mustard, lemon juice, lemon zest, tarragon, salt, and pepper until the mixture is well combined. Set aside.

2. Cook asparagus in the microwave on High until bright green and just tender, 1 to 1 1/2 minutes. Set the asparagus spears aside. Place a chicken breast between two sheets of heavy plastic (resealable freezer bags work well) on a solid, level surface. Firmly pound the chicken breast with the smooth side of a meat mallet to a thickness of about 1/4 inch. Repeat with the rest of the chicken breasts.
3. Place 1 slice of provolone on each chicken breast, and top the cheese with 4 asparagus spears per breast. Roll the chicken breasts around the asparagus and cheese, making a tidy package, and place, seam sides down, in the prepared baking dish. With a pastry brush, apply a coating of the mayonnaise mixture to each chicken breast, and sprinkle each with panko crumbs, pressing the crumbs into the chicken to make a coating.
4. Bake in the preheated oven until the crumbs are browned and the chicken juices run clear, about 25 minutes.

PERFECT TEN BAKED COD

Servings: 4 | Prep: 10m | Cooks: 25m | Total: 35m

NUTRITION FACTS

Calories: 280 | Carbohydrates: 9.3g | Fat: 16.1g | Protein: 20.9g | Cholesterol: 71mg

INGREDIENTS

- 2 tablespoons butter
- 1/4 cup dry white wine
- 1/2 sleeve buttery round crackers (such as Ritz), crushed
- 1 tablespoon chopped fresh parsley
- 2 tablespoons butter
- 1 tablespoon chopped green onion
- 1 pound thick-cut cod loin
- 1 lemon, cut into wedges
- 1/2 lemon, juiced

DIRECTIONS

1. Preheat oven to 400 degrees F (200 degrees C).
2. Place 2 tablespoons butter in a microwave-safe bowl; melt in microwave on high, about 30 seconds. Stir buttery round crackers into melted butter.
3. Place remaining 2 tablespoons butter in a 7x11-inch baking dish. Melt in the preheated oven, 1 to 3 minutes. Remove dish from oven.
4. Coat both sides of cod in melted butter in the baking dish.
5. Bake cod in the preheated oven for 10 minutes. Remove from oven; top with lemon juice, wine, and cracker mixture. Place back in oven and bake until fish is opaque and flakes easily with a fork, about 10 more minutes.
6. Garnish baked cod with parsley and green onion. Serve with lemon wedges.

OLD-FASHIONED PANCAKES

Servings: 4 | Prep: 5m | Cooks: 20m | Total: 25m

NUTRITION FACTS

Calories: 318 | Carbohydrates: 43.7g | Fat: 11.9g | Protein: 9g | Cholesterol: 75mg

INGREDIENTS

- 1 1/2 cups all-purpose flour
- 3 tablespoons butter, melted
- 3 1/2 teaspoons baking powder
- 1 egg
- 1 teaspoon salt
- 1 1/4 cups milk
- 1 tablespoon white sugar
- cooking spray

DIRECTIONS

1. Sift together flour, baking powder, salt, and sugar in a large bowl.
2. Whisk in melted butter, egg, and milk until combined. Let batter rest for 5 minutes.
3. Preheat a large skillet over medium-high heat. Spray with cooking spray. Pour batter into the hot skillet, about 1/4 cup of batter for each pancake. Cook for 2 to 3 minutes, until bubbles appear on the sides and center of each pancake. Flip and cook until golden, about 1 to 2 minutes.

BROCCOLI, RICE, CHEESE, AND CHICKEN CASSEROLE

Servings: 8 | Prep: 15m | Cooks: 30m | Total: 45m

NUTRITION FACTS

Calories: 756.1 | Carbohydrates: 82.7g | Protein: 36g | Cholesterol: 109.5mg

INGREDIENTS

- 2 cups water
- 1/4 cup butter
- 2 cups uncooked instant rice
- 1 cup milk
- 2 (10 ounce) cans chunk chicken, drained
- 1 (16 ounce) package frozen chopped broccoli
- 1 (10.75 ounce) can condensed cream of mushroom soup
- 1 small white onion, chopped
- 1 (10.75 ounce) can condensed cream of chicken soup

- 1 pound processed cheese food

DIRECTIONS

1. Preheat oven to 350 degrees F (175 degrees C).
2. In a medium saucepan, bring the water to a boil. Mix in the instant rice, cover, and remove from heat. Let stand 5 minutes.
3. In a 9x13 inch baking dish, mix the prepared rice, chicken, cream of mushroom soup, cream of chicken soup, butter, milk, broccoli, onion, and processed cheese.
4. Bake in the preheated oven for 30 to 35 minutes, or until cheese is melted. Stir halfway through cooking to help cheese melt evenly.

SLIDER-STYLE MINI BURGERS
Servings: 24 | Prep: 10m | Cooks: 40m | Total: 50m

NUTRITION FACTS

Calories: 232 | Carbohydrates: 16.1g | Fat: 13.2g | Protein: 12g | Cholesterol: 36mg

INGREDIENTS

- 2 pounds ground beef
- 2 cups shredded Cheddar cheese
- 1 (1.25 ounce) envelope onion soup mix
- 24 dinner rolls, split
- 1/2 cup mayonnaise
- 1/2 cup sliced pickles (optional)

DIRECTIONS

1. Preheat an oven to 350 degrees F (175 degrees C). Cover a baking sheet with aluminum foil and spray with cooking spray.
2. Mix together the ground beef and onion soup mix in a large skillet; cook and stir over medium-high heat until the beef is crumbly, evenly browned, and no longer pink. Drain and discard any excess grease. Remove from heat. Stir the mayonnaise and Cheddar cheese into the ground beef mixture.
3. Lay the bottoms of the dinner rolls on the prepared baking sheet. Spread the cheese and beef mixture on the bottom half of each roll. Replace the tops. Cover with another sheet of aluminum foil sprayed with cooking spray.
4. ake in the preheated oven until the burgers are heated through and cheese melts, about 30 minutes. Serve with sliced pickles.

POTATO CHIPS
Servings: 4 | Prep: 30m | Cooks: 5m | Total: 35m

NUTRITION FACTS

Calories: 80 | Carbohydrates: 11.6g | Fat: 3.5g | Protein: 1.2g | Cholesterol: 0mg

INGREDIENTS

- 1 tablespoon vegetable oil
- 1 potato, sliced paper thin (peel optional)
- 1/2 teaspoon salt, or to taste

DIRECTIONS

1. Pour the vegetable oil into a plastic bag (a produce bag works well). Add the potato slices, and shake to coat.
2. Coat a large dinner plate lightly with oil or cooking spray. Arrange potato slices in a single layer on the dish.
3. Cook in the microwave for 3 to 5 minutes, or until lightly browned (if not browned, they will not become crisp). Times will vary depending on the power of your microwave. Remove chips from plate, and toss with salt (or other seasonings). Let cool. Repeat process with the remaining potato slices. You will not need to keep oiling the plate.

BEST GREEN BEAN CASSEROLE

Servings: 6 | Prep: 10m | Cooks: 15m | Total: 25m

NUTRITION FACTS

Calories: 322 | Carbohydrates: 20.2g | Fat: 23.2g | Protein: 6.6g | Cholesterol: 20mg

INGREDIENTS

- 2 (14.5 ounce) cans green beans, drained
- 1 (6 ounce) can French fried onions
- 1 (10.75 ounce) can condensed cream of mushroom soup
- 1 cup shredded Cheddar cheese

DIRECTIONS

1. Preheat oven to 350 degrees F (175 degrees C).
2. Place green beans and soup in a large microwave-safe bowl. Mix well and heat in the microwave on HIGH until warm (3 to 5 minutes). Stir in 1/2 cup of cheese and heat mixture for another 2 to 3 minutes. Transfer green bean mixture to a casserole dish and sprinkle with French fried onions and remaining cheese.
3. Bake in a preheated 350 degrees F (175 degrees C) oven until the cheese melts and the onions just begin to brown.

AIMEE'S QUICK CHICKEN

Servings: 4 | Prep: 5m | Cooks: 30m | Total: 35m

NUTRITION FACTS

Calories: 242.5 | Carbohydrates: 8.8g | Protein: 32.4g | Cholesterol: 81mg

INGREDIENTS

- 4 skinless, boneless chicken breast halves
- 1/4 cup bacon bits
- 4 ounces Dijon mustard
- 1/2 cup grated Parmesan cheese
- 1/4 cup teriyaki sauce

DIRECTIONS

1. Preheat oven to 400 degrees F (200 degrees C).
2. Place chicken in a 9x13 inch baking dish. Slather mustard evenly over chicken, then pour teriyaki sauce evenly over all. Sprinkle with bacon bits, then cover with cheese.
3. Bake at 400 degrees F (200 degrees C) for 30 minutes.

EASY QUICHE

Servings: 8 | Prep: 10m | Cooks: 50m | Total: 1h

NUTRITION FACTS

Calories: 371 | Carbohydrates: 12.5g | Fat: 26.6g | Protein: 21g | Cholesterol: 161mg

INGREDIENTS

- 2 cups milk
- 1 cup grated Parmesan cheese
- 4 eggs
- 1 (10 ounce) package chopped frozen broccoli, thawed and drained
- 3/4 cup biscuit baking mix
- 1 cup cubed cooked ham
- 1/4 cup butter, softened
- 8 ounces shredded Cheddar cheese

DIRECTIONS

1. Preheat oven to 375 degrees F (190 degrees C). Lightly grease a 10 inch quiche dish.
2. In a large bowl, beat together milk, eggs, baking mix, butter and parmesan cheese. Batter will be lumpy. Stir in broccoli, ham and Cheddar cheese. Pour into prepared quiche dish.

3. Bake in preheated oven for 50 minutes, until eggs are set and top is golden brown.

AWESOME HONEY PECAN PORK CHOPS
Servings: 4 | Prep: 15m | Cooks: 10m | Total: 25m

NUTRITION FACTS

Calories: 518 | Carbohydrates: 30.3g | Fat: 30.7g | Protein: 30.6g | Cholesterol: 100mg

INGREDIENTS

- 1 1/4 pounds boneless pork loin, pounded thin
- 2 tablespoons butter
- 1/2 cup all-purpose flour for coating
- 1/4 cup honey
- salt and pepper to taste
- 1/4 cup chopped pecans

DIRECTIONS

1. In a shallow dish, mix together flour, salt and pepper. Dredge pork cutlets in the flour mixture.
2. In a large skillet, melt butter over medium-high heat. Add chops, and brown both sides. Transfer to a warm plate.
3. Mix honey and pecans into the pan drippings. Heat through, stirring constantly. Pour sauce over cutlets.

BEEF NACHO CASSEROLE
Servings: 6 | Prep: 15m | Cooks: 20m | Total: 35m

NUTRITION FACTS

Calories: 497 | Carbohydrates: 23.9g | Fat: 33.6g | Protein: 26.1g | Cholesterol: 98mg

INGREDIENTS

- 1 pound ground beef
- 1 teaspoon chili powder
- 1 1/2 cups chunky salsa
- 2 cups crushed tortilla chips
- 1 (10 ounce) can whole kernel corn, drained
- 2 cups Colby cheese
- 3/4 cup creamy salad dressing (e.g. Miracle Whip)

DIRECTIONS

1. Preheat the oven to 350 degrees F (175 degrees C).
2. Place ground beef in a large skillet over medium-high heat. Cook, stirring to crumble, until evenly browned. Drain grease. Remove from the heat, and stir the salsa, corn, mayonnaise and chili powder into the beef. In a 2 quart casserole dish, layer the ground beef mixture, tortilla chips and cheese twice, ending with cheese on top.
3. Bake for 20 minutes uncovered in the preheated oven, until cheese is melted and dish is thoroughly heated.

FAJITA SEASONING

Servings: 4 | Prep: 5m | Cooks: 0m | Total: 5m

NUTRITION FACTS

Calories: 21 | Carbohydrates: 4.6g | Fat: 0.4g | Protein: 0.4g | Cholesterol: 0mg

INGREDIENTS

- 1 tablespoon cornstarch
- 1/2 teaspoon onion powder
- 2 teaspoons chili powder
- 1/2 teaspoon garlic powder
- 1 teaspoon salt
- 1/4 teaspoon cayenne pepper
- 1 teaspoon paprika
- 1/2 teaspoon ground cumin
- 1 teaspoon white sugar

DIRECTIONS

1. Stir cornstarch, chili powder, salt, paprika, sugar, onion powder, garlic powder, cayenne pepper, and cumin together in a small bowl.

GREEN BEANS WITH CHERRY TOMATOES

Servings: 6 | Prep: 5m | Cooks: 15m | Total: 20m

NUTRITION FACTS

Calories: 122 | Carbohydrates: 12.6g | Fat: 8g | Protein: 2.6g | Cholesterol: 20mg

INGREDIENTS

- 1 1/2 pounds green beans, trimmed and cut into 2 inch pieces
- 3/4 teaspoon garlic salt

- 1 1/2 cups water
- 1/4 teaspoon pepper
- 1/4 cup butter
- 1 1/2 teaspoons chopped fresh basil
- 1 tablespoon sugar
- 2 cups cherry tomato halves

DIRECTIONS

1. Place beans and water in a large saucepan. Cover, and bring to a boil. Set heat to low, and simmer until tender, about 10 minutes. Drain off water, and set aside.
2. Melt butter in a skillet over medium heat. Stir in sugar, garlic salt, pepper and basil. Add tomatoes, and cook stirring gently just until soft. Pour the tomato mixture over the green beans, and toss gently to blend.

PERFECT MASHED POTATOES

Servings: 4 | Prep: 20m | Cooks: 20m | Total: 40m

NUTRITION FACTS

Calories: 333 | Carbohydrates: 49.7g | Fat: 12.7g | Protein: 6.7g | Cholesterol: 34mg

INGREDIENTS

- 3 large russet potatoes, peeled and cut in half lengthwise
- 1/4 cup butter
- 1/2 cup whole milk
- salt and ground black pepper to taste

DIRECTIONS

1. Place the potatoes into a large pot, and cover with salted water. Bring to a boil, reduce heat to medium-low, cover, and simmer until tender, 20 to 25 minutes. Drain, and return the potatoes to the pot. Turn heat to high, and allow the potatoes to dry for about 30 seconds. Turn off the heat.
2. Mash the potatoes with a potato masher twice around the pot, then add the butter and milk. Continue to mash until smooth and fluffy. Whisk in the salt and black pepper until evenly distributed, about 15 seconds.

EASY SAUSAGE GRAVY AND BISCUITS

Servings: 8 | Prep: 5m | Cooks: 10m | Total: 15m

NUTRITION FACTS

Calories: 333 | Carbohydrates: 30.8g | Fat: 18.7g | Protein: 9.8g | Cholesterol: 25mg

INGREDIENTS

- 1 (16 ounce) can refrigerated jumbo buttermilk biscuits
- 2 1/2 cups milk
- 1 (9.6 ounce) package Jimmy Dean Original Hearty Pork Sausage Crumbles
- Salt and ground black pepper to taste
- 1/4 cup flour

DIRECTIONS

1. Bake biscuits according to package directions.
2. Meanwhile, cook sausage in large skillet over medium heat 5-6 minutes or until thoroughly heated, stirring frequently. Stir in flour. Gradually add milk; cook until mixture comes to a boil and thickens, stirring constantly. Reduce heat to medium-low; simmer 2 minutes, stirring constantly. Season to taste with salt and pepper.
3. Split biscuits in half. Place 2 halves on each of 8 plates; top with about 1/3 cup gravy.

FIERY FISH TACOS WITH CRUNCHY CORN SALSA

Servings: 6 | Prep: 30m | Cooks: 10m | Total: 40m

NUTRITION FACTS

Calories: 351 | Carbohydrates: 40.3g | Fat: 9.6g | Protein: 28.7g | Cholesterol: 43mg

INGREDIENTS

- 2 cups cooked corn kernels
- 1 tablespoon ground black pepper
- 1/2 cup diced red onion
- 2 tablespoons salt, or to taste
- 1 cup peeled, diced jicama
- 6 (4 ounce) fillets tilapia
- 1/2 cup diced red bell pepper
- 2 tablespoons olive oil
- 1 cup fresh cilantro leaves, chopped
- 12 corn tortillas, warmed
- 1 lime, juiced and zested
- 2 tablespoons sour cream, or to taste
- 2 tablespoons cayenne pepper, or to taste

DIRECTIONS

1. Preheat grill for high heat.

2. In a medium bowl, mix together corn, red onion, jicama, red bell pepper, and cilantro. Stir in lime juice and zest.
3. In a small bowl, combine cayenne pepper, ground black pepper, and salt.
4. Brush each fillet with olive oil, and sprinkle with spices to taste.
5. Arrange fillets on grill grate, and cook for 3 minutes per side. For each fiery fish taco, top two corn tortillas with fish, sour cream, and corn salsa.

EGG AND SAUSAGE CASSEROLE

Servings: 12 | Prep: 15m | Cooks: 35m | Total: 50m

NUTRITION FACTS

Calories: 341 | Carbohydrates: 8.7g | Fat: 24.7g | Protein: 19.9g | Cholesterol: 177mg

INGREDIENTS

- 1 pound pork sausage
- 2 cups shredded mozzarella cheese
- 1 (8 ounce) package refrigerated crescent roll dough
- 2 cups shredded Cheddar cheese
- 8 eggs, beaten
- 1 teaspoon dried oregano

DIRECTIONS

1. Place sausage in a large, deep skillet. Cook over medium-high heat until evenly brown. Drain, crumble, and set aside.
2. Preheat oven to 325 degrees F (165 degrees C). Lightly grease a 9x13 inch baking dish.
3. Line the bottom of the prepared baking dish with crescent roll dough, and sprinkle with crumbled sausage. In a large bowl, mix beaten eggs, mozzarella, and Cheddar. Season the mixture with oregano, and pour over the sausage and crescent rolls.
4. Bake 25 to 30 minutes in the preheated oven, or until a knife inserted in the center comes out clean.

FRIED CABBAGE

Servings: 6 | Prep: 20m | Cooks: 25m | Total: 45m

NUTRITION FACTS

Calories: 47 | Carbohydrates: 5.2g | Fat: 2g | Protein: 2.8g | Cholesterol: 5mg

INGREDIENTS

- 3 slices bacon, chopped
- 1 pinch white sugar

- 1/4 cup chopped onion
- salt and pepper to taste
- 6 cups cabbage, cut into thin wedges
- 1 tablespoon cider vinegar
- 2 tablespoons water

DIRECTIONS

1. Place bacon in a large, deep skillet. Cook over medium-high heat until evenly brown. Remove bacon, and set aside.
2. Cook onion in the hot bacon grease until tender. Add cabbage, and stir in water, sugar, salt, and pepper. Cook until cabbage wilts, about 15 minutes. Stir in bacon. Splash with vinegar before serving.

CHINESE PEPPER STEAK

Servings: 4 | Prep: 15m | Cooks: 15m | Total: 30m

NUTRITION FACTS

Calories: 312 | Carbohydrates: 17g | Fat: 15.4g | Protein: 26.1g | Cholesterol: 69mg

INGREDIENTS

- 1 pound beef top sirloin steak
- 3 tablespoons vegetable oil, divided
- 1/4 cup soy sauce
- 1 red onion, cut into 1-inch squares
- 2 tablespoons white sugar
- 1 green bell pepper, cut into 1-inch squares
- 2 tablespoons cornstarch
- 2 tomatoes, cut into wedges
- 1/2 teaspoon ground ginger

DIRECTIONS

1. Slice the steak into 1/2-inch thick slices across the grain.
2. Whisk together soy sauce, sugar, cornstarch, and ginger in a bowl until the sugar has dissolved and the mixture is smooth. Place the steak slices into the marinade, and stir until well-coated.
3. Heat 1 tablespoon of vegetable oil in a wok or large skillet over medium-high heat, and place 1/3 of the steak strips into the hot oil. Cook and stir until the beef is well-browned, about 3 minutes, and remove the beef from the wok to a bowl. Repeat twice more, with the remaining beef, and set the cooked beef aside.
4. Return all the cooked beef to the hot wok, and stir in the onion. Toss the beef and onion together until the onion begins to soften, about 2 minutes, then stir in the green pepper. Cook and stir the

mixture until the pepper has turned bright green and started to become tender, about 2 minutes, then add the tomatoes, stir everything together, and serve.

ONE PAN ORECCHIETTE PASTA

Servings: 2 | Prep: 15m | Cooks: 25m | Total: 40m

NUTRITION FACTS

Calories: 662 | Carbohydrates: 46.2g | Fat: 39.1g | Protein: 31.2g | Cholesterol: 60mg

INGREDIENTS

- 2 tablespoons olive oil
- 3 1/2 cups low-sodium chicken broth, divided, or as needed
- 1/2 onion, diced
- 1 1/4 cups orecchiette pasta, or more to taste
- salt to taste
- 1/2 cup roughly chopped arugula, or to taste
- 8 ounces spicy Italian sausages, casings removed
- 1/4 cup finely grated Parmigiano-Reggiano cheese, or to taste

DIRECTIONS

1. Heat olive oil in a large, deep skillet over medium heat. Cook and stir onion with a pinch of salt in hot oil until onion is soft and golden, 5 to 7 minutes. Stir sausage into onions; cook and stir until sausage is broken up and browned, 5 to 7 minutes.
2. Pour 1 1/2 cups chicken broth into sausage mixture and bring to a boil while scraping the browned bits of food off of the bottom of the pan with a wooden spoon. Add orecchiette pasta; cook and stir pasta in hot broth, adding remaining broth when liquid is absorbed, until pasta is cooked through and most of the broth is absorbed, about 15 minutes.
3. Stir arugula into pasta-sausage mixture until arugula wilts. Ladle pasta into bowls and dust with Parmigiano-Reggiano cheese.

CHRIS' BAY AREA BURGER

Servings: 4 | Prep: 10m | Cooks: 20m | Total: 30m

NUTRITION FACTS

Calories: 393 | Carbohydrates: 22.6g | Fat: 22.6g | Protein: 22.9g | Cholesterol: 71mg

INGREDIENTS

- 1 pound ground beef
- 1 teaspoon freshly ground black pepper

- 2 cloves garlic, minced
- 1/2 teaspoon dried basil leaves
- 2 tablespoons extra virgin olive oil
- 4 hamburger buns, split
- 1 1/2 teaspoons salt

DIRECTIONS

1. Preheat an outdoor grill for high heat. Mix together the ground beef, garlic, olive oil, salt, pepper, and basil. Divide into four balls, and flatten into patties.
2. Cook the patties for about 3 to 5 minutes on each side, or to desired doneness. The internal temperature should be at least 160 degrees F (70 degrees C). Remove from grill and place onto hamburger buns. Top with desired toppings and condiments.

SALSA CHICKEN BURRITO FILLING

Servings: 4 | Prep: 5m | Cooks: 30m | Total: 35m

NUTRITION FACTS

Calories: 107.1 | Carbohydrates: 9.6g | Protein: 12.3g | Cholesterol: 30.4mg

INGREDIENTS

- 2 skinless, boneless chicken breast halves
- 1 teaspoon ground cumin
- 1 (4 ounce) can tomato sauce
- 2 cloves garlic, minced
- 1/4 cup salsa
- 1 teaspoon chili powder
- 1 (1.25 ounce) package taco seasoning mix
- hot sauce to taste

DIRECTIONS

1. Place chicken breasts and tomato sauce in a medium saucepan over medium high heat. Bring to a boil, then add the salsa, seasoning, cumin, garlic and chili powder. Let simmer for 15 minutes.
2. With a fork, start pulling the chicken meat apart into thin strings. Keep cooking pulled chicken meat and sauce, covered, for another 5 to 10 minutes. Add hot sauce to taste and stir together (Note: You may need to add a bit of water if the mixture is cooked too high and gets too thick.)

GARLIC CHICKEN WITH ORZO NOODLES

Servings: 4 | Prep: 15m | Cooks: 15m | Total: 30m

NUTRITION FACTS

Calories: 350.7 | Carbohydrates: 40.4g | Protein: 22.3g | Cholesterol: 38.1mg

INGREDIENTS

- 1 cup uncooked orzo pasta
- 1/8 teaspoon salt to taste
- 2 tablespoons olive oil
- 1 tablespoon chopped fresh parsley
- 2 cloves garlic
- 2 cups fresh spinach leaves
- 1/4 teaspoon crushed red pepper
- 2 tablespoons grated Parmesan cheese for topping
- 2 skinless, boneless chicken breast halves - cut into bite-size pieces

DIRECTIONS

1. Bring a large pot of lightly salted water to a boil. Add orzo pasta, cook for 8 to 10 minutes, until al dente, and drain.
2. Heat the oil in a skillet over medium-high heat, and cook the garlic and red pepper 1 minute, until garlic is golden brown. Stir in chicken, season with salt, and cook 2 to 5 minutes, until lightly browned and juices run clear. Reduce heat to medium, and mix in the parsley and cooked orzo. Place spinach in the skillet. Continue cooking 5 minutes, stirring occasionally, until spinach is wilted. Serve topped with Parmesan cheese.

CREAMY HERBED PORK CHOPS

Servings: 4 | Prep: 10m | Cooks: 25m | Total: 35m

NUTRITION FACTS

Calories: 601 | Carbohydrates: 10.9g | Fat: 43.6g | Protein: 40.3g | Cholesterol: 165mg

INGREDIENTS

- 4 thick-cut pork chops
- 1 tablespoon dried basil
- 1 teaspoon Montreal steak seasoning, or to taste
- 1 teaspoon instant beef bouillon granules
- 1/2 cup butter, divided
- 1 teaspoon freshly ground black pepper
- 2 1/2 tablespoons all-purpose flour, or as needed
- 2 cups milk

DIRECTIONS

1. Season pork chops on all sides with Montreal steak seasoning.
2. Melt 2 tablespoons butter in a large skillet over medium heat. Cook chops in melted butter until browned and slightly pink in the center, about 7 to 10 minutes per side. An instant-read thermometer inserted into the center should read at least 145 degrees F (63 degrees C). Add remaining butter to the pan as needed so that about 3 tablespoons pan drippings remain in the pan when the chops are finished cooking. Transfer pork chops to a plate and return skillet to medium-high heat.
3. Mix flour, basil, and beef bouillon together in a bowl. Stir black pepper into skillet with the pan drippings and cook for 1 minute. Add flour mixture and cook, stirring constantly, until browned, about 2 minutes. Pour milk into flour mixture; cook and stir constantly until mixture is thick and bubbly, 4 to 6 minutes. Pour sauce over pork chops and serve.

SWEET AND SOUR SAUCE
Servings: 16 | Prep: 2m | Cooks: 10m | Total: 12m

NUTRITION FACTS

Calories: 43 | Carbohydrates: 10.8g | Fat: 0g | Protein: 0.3g | Cholesterol: 0mg

INGREDIENTS

- 3/4 cup white sugar
- 1/4 cup soy sauce
- 1/3 cup white vinegar
- 1 tablespoon ketchup
- 2/3 cup water
- 2 tablespoons cornstarch

DIRECTIONS

1. Place the sugar, vinegar, water, soy sauce, ketchup and cornstarch in a medium saucepan, and bring to a boil. Stir continuously until the mixture has thickened.

SIMPLE BEEF STROGANOFF
Servings: 4 | Prep: 20m | Cooks: 10m | Total: 30m

NUTRITION FACTS

Calories: 679 | Carbohydrates: 48.2g | Fat: 40.5g | Protein: 28.7g | Cholesterol: 159mg

INGREDIENTS

- 1 (8 ounce) package egg noodles

- 1 tablespoon garlic powder
- 1 pound ground beef
- 1/2 cup sour cream
- 1 (10.75 ounce) can fat free condensed cream of mushroom soup
- salt and pepper to taste

DIRECTIONS

1. Prepare the egg noodles according to package directions and set aside.
2. In a separate large skillet over medium heat, saute the ground beef over medium heat for 5 to 10 minutes, or until browned. Drain the fat and add the soup and garlic powder. Simmer for 10 minutes, stirring occasionally.
3. Remove from heat and combine the meat mixture with the egg noodles. Add the sour cream, stirring well, and season with salt and pepper to taste.

SWEET AND SPICY GREEN BEANS

Servings: 4 | Prep: 15m | Cooks: 10m | Total: 25m

NUTRITION FACTS

Calories: 59 | Carbohydrates: 8.6g | Fat: 2.4g | Protein: 2.1g | Cholesterol: 0mg

INGREDIENTS

- 3/4 pound fresh green beans, trimmed
- 1 teaspoon garlic chili sauce
- 2 tablespoons soy sauce
- 1 teaspoon honey
- 1 clove garlic, minced
- 2 teaspoons canola oil

DIRECTIONS

1. Arrange a steamer basket in a pot over boiling water, and steam the green beans 3 to 4 minutes.
2. In a bowl, mix the soy sauce, garlic, garlic chili sauce, and honey.
3. Heat the canola oil in a skillet over medium heat. Add the green beans, and fry for 3 to 5 minutes. Pour in the soy sauce mixture. Continue cooking and stirring 2 minutes, or until the liquid is nearly evaporated. Serve immediately.

PORTOBELLO PENNE PASTA CASSEROLE

Servings: 8 | Prep: 15m | Cooks: 30m | Total: 45m

NUTRITION FACTS

Calories: 380 | Carbohydrates: 32.1g | Fat: 21.3g | Protein: 16g | Cholesterol: 23mg

INGREDIENTS

- 1 (8 ounce) package uncooked penne pasta
- 1/2 teaspoon dried basil
- 2 tablespoons vegetable oil
- 2 cups milk
- 1/2 pound portobello mushrooms, thinly sliced
- 2 cups shredded mozzarella cheese
- 1/2 cup margarine
- 1 (10 ounce) package frozen chopped spinach, thawed
- 1/4 cup all-purpose flour
- 1/4 cup soy sauce
- 1 large clove garlic, minced

DIRECTIONS

1. Preheat oven to 350 degrees F (175 degrees C). Lightly grease a 9x13 inch baking dish.
2. Bring a large pot of lightly salted water to a boil. Place pasta in the pot, cook for 8 to 10 minutes, until al dente, and drain.
3. Heat the oil in a saucepan over medium heat. Stir in the mushrooms, cook 1 minute, and set aside. Melt margarine in the saucepan. Mix in flour, garlic, and basil. Gradually mix in milk until thickened. Stir in 1 cup cheese until melted. Remove saucepan from heat, and mix in cooked pasta, mushrooms, spinach, and soy sauce. Transfer to the prepared baking dish, and top with remaining cheese.
4. Bake 20 minutes in the preheated oven, until bubbly and lightly brown.

CANDIED CARROTS

Servings: 4 | Prep: 10m | Cooks: 30m | Total: 40m

NUTRITION FACTS

Calories: 150 | Carbohydrates: 24.5g | Fat: 6g | Protein: 1.2g | Cholesterol: 15mg

INGREDIENTS

- 1 pound carrots, cut into 2 inch pieces
- 1 pinch salt
- 2 tablespoons butter, diced
- 1 pinch ground black pepper
- 1/4 cup packed brown sugar

DIRECTIONS

1. Place carrots in a pot of salted water. Bring water to a boil, reduce heat to a high simmer and cook about 20 to 30 minutes. Do not cook the carrots to a mushy stage!
2. Drain the carrots, reduce the heat to its lowest possible setting and return the carrots to the pan. Stir in butter, brown sugar, salt and pepper. Cook for about 3 to 5 minutes, until sugar is bubbly. Serve hot.

BAKED CHICKEN WINGS
Servings: 2 | Prep: 10m | Cooks: 1h | Total: 1h10m

NUTRITION FACTS

Calories: 532.1 | Carbohydrates: 3.9g | Protein: 31.7g | Cholesterol: 96.6mg

INGREDIENTS

- 3 tablespoons olive oil
- 1 teaspoon garlic powder
- 3 cloves garlic, pressed
- 1 pinch salt and ground black pepper to taste
- 2 teaspoons chili powder
- 10 eaches chicken wings

DIRECTIONS

1. Preheat the oven to 375 degrees F (190 degrees C).
2. Combine the olive oil, garlic, chili powder, garlic powder, salt, and pepper in a large, resealable bag; seal and shake to combine. Add the chicken wings; reseal and shake to coat. Arrange the chicken wings on a baking sheet.
3. Cook the wings in the preheated oven 1 hour, or until crisp and cooked through.

EASY CARAMELIZED ONION PORK CHOPS
Servings: 4 | Prep: 5m | Cooks: 40m | Total: 45m

NUTRITION FACTS

Calories: 47 | Carbohydrates: 4g | Fat: 3.5g | Protein: 0.5g | Cholesterol: 0mg

INGREDIENTS

- 1 tablespoon vegetable oil
- 2 teaspoons ground black pepper
- 4 (4 ounce) pork loin chops, 1/2 inch thick
- 1 onion, cut into strips
- 3 teaspoons seasoning salt

- 1 cup water

DIRECTIONS

1. Rub chops with 2 teaspoons seasoning salt and 1 teaspoon pepper, or to taste.
2. In a skillet, heat oil over medium heat. Brown pork chops on each side. Add the onions and water to the pan. Cover, reduce heat, and simmer for 20 minutes.
3. Turn chops over, and add remaining salt and pepper. Cover, and cook until water evaporates and onions turn light to medium brown. Remove chops from pan, and serve with onions on top.

TATER TOT TACO CASSEROLE
Servings: 8 | Prep: 15m | Cooks: 1h | Total: 1h15m

NUTRITION FACTS

Calories: 477 | Carbohydrates: 38.4g | Fat: 27g | Protein: 24.9g | Cholesterol: 76mg

INGREDIENTS

- 1 pound ground beef
- 1 (12 ounce) can black beans, rinsed and drained
- 1 small onion, diced
- 1 (12 ounce) bag shredded Mexican cheese blend
- 1 clove garlic, minced
- 1 (16 ounce) package frozen tater tots
- 1 (1 ounce) packet taco seasoning mix
- 1 (12 fluid ounce) can enchilada sauce
- 1 (16 ounce) bag frozen Mexican-style corn

DIRECTIONS

1. Preheat an oven to 375 degrees F (190 degrees C). Prepare a 9x13-inch baking dish with cooking spray.
2. Cook the ground beef in a skillet over medium heat until completely browned, 5 to 7 minutes. Add the onion, garlic, taco seasoning mix, frozen Mexican-style corn, and black beans to the ground beef; cook and stir another 10 minutes. Set aside to cool slightly.
3. Combine the ground beef mixture in a large bowl with about 3/4 of the Mexican cheese blend and the tater tots; stir to combine.
4. Pour about 1/3 of the enchilada sauce into the bottom of the prepared baking dish. Add the tater tot mixture to the baking dish; lightly pat the mixture down into a solid, even layer. Pour the remaining enchilada sauce over the tater tot layer.
5. Bake in the preheated oven for 40 minutes. Sprinkle the remaining Mexican cheese over the casserole and return to oven until the cheese is melted and bubbly, about 5 minutes more.

BACON FOR THE FAMILY OR A CROWD

Servings: 4 | Prep: 5m | Cooks: 15m | Total: 20m

NUTRITION FACTS

Calories: 203 | Carbohydrates: 0.5g | Fat: 15.6g | Protein: 13.9g | Cholesterol: 41mg

INGREDIENTS

- 1 pound thick sliced bacon

DIRECTIONS

1. Preheat oven to 350 degrees F (175 degrees C). Line a baking sheet with aluminum foil. Arrange bacon on baking sheet in a single layer with the edges touching or slightly overlapping.
2. Bake in preheated oven to desired degree of doneness, 10 to 15 minutes. Remove bacon from the baking sheet with tongs or a fork, and drain on a paper towel-lined plate.

KIELBASA AND CABBAGE

Servings: 6 | Prep: 10m | Cooks: 30m | Total: 40m

NUTRITION FACTS

Calories: 377 | Carbohydrates: 20.2g | Fat: 26g | Protein: 17.2g | Cholesterol: 63mg

INGREDIENTS

- 6 slices bacon
- 1/4 teaspoon crushed red pepper flakes
- 1/4 cup water
- 1/4 teaspoon seasoning salt
- 2 tablespoons white sugar
- 3 teaspoons caraway seed
- 1 onion, chopped
- 1 large head cabbage, cut into small wedges
- 2 teaspoons minced garlic
- 1 pound Polish kielbasa

DIRECTIONS

1. In a large skillet, fry bacon over medium high heat until browned, turning once. Remove bacon from pan, reserving drippings, and place on paper towels.
2. Stir water, sugar, onions, garlic, red pepper flakes, seasoned salt, and caraway seeds into drippings. Add cabbage, and gently stir. Cover, and cook over medium heat for 10 to 15 minutes.

3. Add kielbasa to the pan. Cook, covered, for an additional 10 to 15 minutes. Crumble bacon over top, and serve hot.

CAMPBELL'S GREEN BEAN CASSEROLE

Servings: 12 | Prep: 10m | Cooks: 30m | Total: 40m

INGREDIENTS

- 2 (10.75 ounce) cans Campbell's Condensed Cream of Mushroom Soup or Campbell's Condensed 98% Fat Free Cream of Mushroom Soup
- 1/4 teaspoon ground black pepper
- 1 cup milk
- 8 cups cooked cut green beans
- 2 teaspoons soy sauce
- 2 2/3 cups French's French Fried Onions

DIRECTIONS

1. Stir soup, milk, soy sauce, pepper, beans and 1 1/3 cups onions in 3-qt. casserole.
2. Bake at 350 degrees F. for 25 min. or until hot. Stir.
3. Top with remaining onions. Bake for 5 min. more.

BARBECUE BEEF CUPS

Servings: 6 | Prep: 15m | Cooks: 25m | Total: 40m

NUTRITION FACTS

Calories: 353 | Carbohydrates: 32.4g | Fat: 17.2g | Protein: 16.5g | Cholesterol: 46mg

INGREDIENTS

- 3/4 pound lean ground beef
- 1 (12 ounce) package refrigerated biscuit dough
- 1/2 cup barbeque sauce
- 1/3 cup shredded Cheddar cheese
- 1 tablespoon dried minced onion

DIRECTIONS

1. Preheat oven to 350 degrees F (175 degrees C). Grease the cups of a muffin pan.
2. In a large heavy skillet over medium heat, cook beef until evenly brown. Drain excess fat. Stir in barbeque sauce and dried onion. Simmer for a few minutes over low heat.
3. Flatten each biscuit, and press into cups of the prepared muffin pan. Make sure the dough comes to the top of the pan. Spoon a portion of the meat mixture into each dough cup.

4. Bake in preheated oven for 12 minutes. Sprinkle with cheese, and bake for 3 more minutes.

GARLIC MASHED CAULIFLOWER

Servings: 4 | Prep: 15m | Cooks: 10m | Total: 25m

NUTRITION FACTS

Calories: 98 | Carbohydrates: 8.4g | Fat: 5.7g | Protein: 5.2g | Cholesterol: 7mg

INGREDIENTS

- 1 tablespoon olive oil
- 1 tablespoon reduced-fat cream cheese
- 1 clove garlic, smashed
- 1/2 teaspoon kosher salt
- 1/4 cup grated Parmesan cheese
- 1/8 teaspoon freshly ground black pepper

DIRECTIONS

1. Place a steamer insert into a saucepan and fill with water to just below the bottom of the steamer. Bring water to a boil. Add cauliflower, cover, and steam until tender, about 10 minutes.
2. Meanwhile, heat olive oil in a small skillet over medium heat; cook and stir garlic until softened, about 2 minutes. Remove from heat.
3. Transfer half the cauliflower to a food processor; cover and blend on high. Add remaining cauliflower florets, one at a time, until vegetables are creamy. Blend in garlic, Parmesan cheese, cream cheese, salt, and black pepper.

UGLIES

Servings: 8 | Prep: 20m | Cooks: 15m | Total: 40m | Additional: 5m

NUTRITION FACTS

Calories: 360 | Carbohydrates: 33.6g | Fat: 17.2g | Protein: 17.2g | Cholesterol: 56mg

INGREDIENTS

- 1 pound ground beef chuck
- 1 ½ cups barbeque sauce
- 1/2 cup chopped onion
- 1 (10 ounce) package refrigerated biscuit dough
- 1/2 teaspoon garlic powder
- 2 cups shredded Cheddar cheese

DIRECTIONS

1. Preheat oven to 400 degrees F (200 degrees C). Lightly grease 8 muffin cups.
2. In a large skillet or frying pan, cook ground chuck with onion and garlic powder until evenly brown; drain off the grease. Stir in the barbeque sauce and simmer for another 3 minutes.
3. Roll out each biscuit on a floured surface so that each biscuit is 6 inches across. Put the biscuit in the muffin tin and fold up sides to create a cup shape. Fill each biscuit fill almost to the top with the meat mixture; top with cheddar cheese.
4. Bake in preheated oven until biscuits are baked, cheese is melted and tops are golden brown, about 15 minutes.

LIME CILANTRO RICE
Servings: 4 | Prep: 10m | Cooks: 20m | Total: 30m

NUTRITION FACTS

Calories: 84 | Carbohydrates: 12.7g | Fat: 3.1g | Protein: 2.4g | Cholesterol: 8mg

INGREDIENTS

- 2 cups water
- 1 teaspoon lime zest
- 1 tablespoon butter
- 2 tablespoons fresh lime juice
- 1 cup long-grain white rice
- 1/2 cup chopped cilantro

DIRECTIONS

1. Bring the water to a boil; stir the butter and rice into the water. Cover, reduce heat to low, and simmer until the rice is tender, about 20 minutes.
2. Stir the lime zest, lime juice, and cilantro into the cooked rice just before serving.

ANDREA'S PASTA FAGIOLI
Servings: 8 | Prep: 10m | Cooks: 1h30m | Total: 1h40m

NUTRITION FACTS

Calories: 403 | Carbohydrates: 68g | Fat: 7.6g | Protein: 16.3g | Cholesterol: 3mg

INGREDIENTS

- 3 tablespoons olive oil
- 1 1/2 teaspoons dried oregano

- 1 onion, quartered then halved
- 1 teaspoon salt
- 2 cloves garlic, minced
- 1 (15 ounce) can cannellini beans
- 1 (29 ounce) can tomato sauce
- 1 (15 ounce) can navy beans
- 5 1/2 cups water
- 1/3 cup grated Parmesan cheese
- 1 tablespoon dried parsley
- 1 pound ditalini pasta
- 1 1/2 teaspoons dried basil

DIRECTIONS

1. In a large pot over medium heat, cook onion in olive oil until translucent. Stir in garlic and cook until tender. Reduce heat, and stir in tomato sauce, water, parsley, basil, oregano, salt, cannelini beans, navy beans and Parmesan. Simmer 1 hour.
2. Bring a large pot of lightly salted water to a boil. Add pasta and cook for 8 to 10 minutes or until al dente; drain. Stir into soup.

QUICK BAKED ZUCCHINI CHIPS

Servings: 4 | Prep: 5m | Cooks: 10m | Total: 15m

NUTRITION FACTS

Calories: 92 | Carbohydrates: 13.8g | Fat: 1.7g | Protein: 6.1g | Cholesterol: 2mg

INGREDIENTS

- 2 medium zucchini, cut into 1/4-inch slices
- 2 tablespoons grated Parmesan cheese
- 1/2 cup seasoned dry bread crumbs
- 2 egg whites
- 1/8 teaspoon ground black pepper

DIRECTIONS

1. Preheat the oven to 475 degrees F (245 degrees C).
2. In one small bowl, stir together the bread crumbs, pepper and Parmesan cheese. Place the egg whites in a separate bowl. Dip zucchini slices into the egg whites, then coat the breadcrumb mixture. Place on a greased baking sheet.
3. Bake for 5 minutes in the preheated oven, then turn over and bake for another 5 to 10 minutes, until browned and crispy.

RANCH BURGERS

Servings: 8 | Prep: 15m | Cooks: 10m | Total: 25m

NUTRITION FACTS

Calories: 268 | Carbohydrates: 7.7g | Fat: 15.2g | Protein: 23.1g | Cholesterol: 98mg

INGREDIENTS

- 2 pounds lean ground beef
- 3/4 cup crushed saltine crackers
- 1 (1 ounce) package ranch dressing mix
- 1 onion, chopped
- 1 egg, lightly beaten

DIRECTIONS

1. Preheat the grill for high heat.
2. In a bowl, mix the ground beef, ranch dressing mix, egg, crushed crackers, and onion. Form into hamburger patties.
3. Lightly oil the grill grate. Place patties on the grill, and cook 5 minutes per side, or until well done.

DIJON-TARRAGON CREAM CHICKEN

Servings: 4 | Prep: 15m | Cooks: 30m | Total: 45m

NUTRITION FACTS

Calories: 310.1 | Carbohydrates: 2.1g | Protein: 27.1g | Cholesterol: 120.3mg

INGREDIENTS

- 1 tablespoon butter
- 1/2 cup heavy cream
- 1 tablespoon olive oil
- 1 tablespoon Dijon mustard
- 4 skinless, boneless chicken breast halves
- 2 teaspoons chopped fresh tarragon
- 1 pinch salt and pepper to taste

DIRECTIONS

1. Melt the butter and heat the oil in a skillet over medium-high heat. Season chicken with salt and pepper, and place in the skillet. Brown on both sides. Reduce heat to medium, cover, and continue cooking 15 minutes, or until chicken juices run clear. Set aside and keep warm.

2. Stir cream into the pan, scraping up brown bits. Mix in mustard and tarragon. Cook and stir 5 minutes, or until thickened. Return chicken to skillet to coat with sauce. Drizzle chicken with remaining sauce to serve.

SPICY CHIPOTLE TURKEY BURGERS

Servings: 4 | Prep: 25m | Cooks: 10m | Total: 35m

NUTRITION FACTS

Calories: 376 | Carbohydrates: 25.8g | Fat: 15.3g | Protein: 33.3g | Cholesterol: 102mg

INGREDIENTS

- 1 pound ground turkey
- 1 teaspoon onion powder
- 1/2 cup finely chopped onion
- 1 teaspoon seasoned salt
- 2 tablespoons chopped fresh cilantro
- 1/4 teaspoon black pepper
- 1 chipotle chile in adobo sauce, finely chopped
- 4 slices mozzarella cheese
- 1 teaspoon garlic powder
- 4 hamburger buns, split and toasted

DIRECTIONS

1. Preheat an outdoor grill for medium-high heat, and lightly oil grate. Place the ground turkey, onion, cilantro, chipotle chile pepper, garlic powder, onion powder, seasoned salt, and black pepper in a mixing bowl; mix well. Form into 4 patties.
2. Cook the hamburgers on the preheated grill until the turkey is no longer pink in the center, about 4 minutes per side. Place the mozzarella slices on the patties 2 minutes before they are ready. Serve on the toasted buns.

CHICKEN AND CORN CHILI

Servings: 6 | Prep: 15m | Cooks: 12h | Total: 12h15m

NUTRITION FACTS

Calories: 187.9 | Carbohydrates: 22.6g | Protein: 20.4g | Cholesterol: 40.6mg

INGREDIENTS

- 4 skinless, boneless chicken breast halves
- 1/4 teaspoon salt to taste

- 1 (16 ounce) jar salsa
- 1/4 teaspoon ground black pepper to taste
- 2 teaspoons garlic powder
- 1 (11 ounce) can Mexican-style corn
- 1 teaspoon ground cumin
- 1 (15 ounce) can pinto beans
- 1 teaspoon chili powder

DIRECTIONS

1. Place chicken and salsa in the slow cooker the night before you want to eat this chili. Season with garlic powder, cumin, chili powder, salt, and pepper. Cook 6 to 8 hours on Low setting.
2. About 3 to 4 hours before you want to eat, shred the chicken with 2 forks. Return the meat to the pot, and continue cooking.
3. Stir the corn and the pinto beans into the slow cooker. Simmer until ready to serve.

OVEN FRESH SEASONED POTATO WEDGES
Servings: 4 | Prep: 10m | Cooks: 25m | Total: 35m

NUTRITION FACTS

Calories: 138 | Carbohydrates: 19.8g | Fat: 4.9g | Protein: 4.3g | Cholesterol: 4mg

INGREDIENTS

- 1/4 cup grated Parmesan cheese
- 1/4 teaspoon ground black pepper
- 1 tablespoon olive oil
- 1/4 teaspoon salt
- 1 teaspoon onion powder
- 2 russet potatoes, scrubbed and cut into eighths
- 1 teaspoon garlic powder

DIRECTIONS

1. Preheat an oven to 425 degrees F (220 degrees C).
2. Place Parmesan cheese, olive oil, onion powder, garlic powder, pepper, salt, and potatoes into a resealable plastic bag. Seal the bag, then shake to coat the potatoes with the seasoning. Spread the potatoes over a baking sheet.
3. Bake in the preheated oven until the potatoes are easily pierced with a fork, about 25 minutes.

CANDIED YAMS
Servings: 6 | Prep: 15m | Cooks: 25m | Total: 40m

NUTRITION FACTS

Calories: 282 | Carbohydrates: 50.7g | Fat: 7.9g | Protein: 2.3g | Cholesterol: 20mg

INGREDIENTS

- 1 (29 ounce) can sweet potatoes
- 1/2 cup brown sugar
- 1/4 cup butter, cut into pieces
- 1 1/2 cups miniature marshmallows

DIRECTIONS

1. Preheat oven to 400 degrees F (200 degrees C).
2. Place sweet potatoes in a medium baking dish. Distribute butter pieces evenly over the sweet potatoes. Sprinkle with brown sugar. Layer with miniature marshmallows.
3. Bake in the preheated oven 25 minutes, or until sweet potatoes are tender and marshmallows have melted.

THE BEST SWEET AND SOUR MEATBALLS

Servings: 4 | Prep: 20m | Cooks: 30m | Total: 1h | Additional: 10m

NUTRITION FACTS

Calories: 516 | Carbohydrates: 67.1g | Fat: 16.8g | Protein: 24.5g | Cholesterol: 122mg

INGREDIENTS

- 1 pound ground beef
- 3 tablespoons all-purpose flour
- 1 egg
- 1 1/2 cups water
- 1/4 cup dry bread crumbs
- 1/4 cup distilled white vinegar
- 1 onion, diced
- 3 tablespoons soy sauce
- 1 cup packed brown sugar

DIRECTIONS

1. In a medium bowl, combine the ground beef, egg, bread crumbs and onion. Mix thoroughly and shape into golf ball-sized balls.
2. In a large skillet over medium heat, gently brown the meatballs and set aside.

3. In a large saucepan, combine the brown sugar, flour, water, white vinegar and soy sauce. Mix thoroughly. Add meatballs and bring to a boil. Reduce heat and simmer, stirring often, for 30 minutes.

ASPARAGUS PARMESAN

Servings: 5 | Prep: 5m | Cooks: 10m | Total: 15m

NUTRITION FACTS

Calories: 199 | Carbohydrates: 4.1g | Fat: 17.2g | Protein: 7.8g | Cholesterol: 19mg

INGREDIENTS

- 1 tablespoon butter
- 3/4 cup grated Parmesan cheese
- 1/4 cup olive oil
- salt and pepper to taste
- 1 pound fresh asparagus spears, trimmed

DIRECTIONS

1. Melt butter with olive oil in a large skillet over medium heat. Add asparagus spears, and cook, stirring occasionally for about 10 minutes, or to desired firmness. Drain off excess oil, and sprinkle with Parmesan cheese, salt and pepper.

SEARED AHI TUNA STEAKS

Servings: 2 | Prep: 5m | Cooks: 12m | Total: 17m

NUTRITION FACTS

Calories: 301 | Carbohydrates: 0.7g | Fat: 17.8g | Protein: 33.3g | Cholesterol: 71mg

INGREDIENTS

- 2 (5 ounce) ahi tuna steaks
- 1/2 tablespoon butter
- 1 teaspoon kosher salt
- 2 tablespoons olive oil
- 1/4 teaspoon cayenne pepper
- 1 teaspoon whole peppercorns

DIRECTIONS

1. Season the tuna steaks with salt and cayenne pepper.

2. Melt the butter with the olive oil in a skillet over medium-high heat. Cook the peppercorns in the mixture until they soften and pop, about 5 minutes. Gently place the seasoned tuna in the skillet and cook to desired doneness, 1 1/2 minutes per side for rare.

BEER BATTER FISH MADE GREAT

Servings: 8 | Prep: 15m | Cooks: 15m | Total: 30m

NUTRITION FACTS

Calories: 447 | Carbohydrates: 22.6g | Fat: 30.2g | Protein: 18.8g | Cholesterol: 68mg

INGREDIENTS

- 2 quarts vegetable oil for frying
- 2 tablespoons paprika
- 8 (4 ounce) fillets cod
- 2 teaspoons salt
- salt and pepper to taste
- 2 teaspoons ground black pepper
- 1 cup all-purpose flour
- 1 egg, beaten
- 2 tablespoons garlic powder
- 1 (12 fluid ounce) can or bottle beer

DIRECTIONS

1. Heat oil in a deep fryer to 365 degrees F (185 degrees C). Rinse fish, pat dry, and season with salt and pepper.
2. Combine flour, garlic powder, paprika, 2 teaspoons salt, and 2 teaspoons pepper. Stir egg into dry ingredients. Gradually mix in beer until a thin batter is formed. You should be able to see the fish through the batter after it has been dipped.
3. Dip fish fillets into the batter, then drop one at a time into hot oil. Fry fish, turning once, until both sides are golden brown. Drain on paper towels, and serve warm.

CARROT RICE

Servings: 6 | Prep: 15m | Cooks: 20m | Total: 35m

NUTRITION FACTS

Calories: 179 | Carbohydrates: 30.1g | Fat: 4.8g | Protein: 4g | Cholesterol: 0mg

INGREDIENTS

- 1 cup basmati rice
- 1 teaspoon minced fresh ginger root

- 2 cups water
- 3/4 cup grated carrots
- 1/4 cup roasted peanuts
- salt to taste
- 1 tablespoon margarine
- cayenne pepper to taste
- 1 onion, sliced
- chopped fresh cilantro

DIRECTIONS

1. Combine rice and water in a medium saucepan. Bring to a boil over high heat. Reduce heat to low, cover with lid, and allow to steam until tender, about 20 minutes.
2. While rice is cooking, grind peanuts in a blender and set aside. Heat the margarine in a skillet over medium heat. Stir in the onion; cook and stir until the onion has softened and turned golden brown about 10 minutes. Stir in ginger, carrots, and salt to taste. Reduce heat to low and cover to steam 5 minutes. Stir in cayenne pepper and peanuts. When rice is done, add it to skillet and stir gently to combine with other ingredients. Garnish with chopped cilantro.

PIZZA PINWHEELS

Servings: 8 | Prep: 20m | Cooks: 12m | Total: 32m

NUTRITION FACTS

Calories: 235 | Carbohydrates: 16.4g | Fat: 13.1g | Protein: 11g | Cholesterol: 24mg

INGREDIENTS

- 1 (8 ounce) can refrigerated crescent roll dough
- 24 slices pepperoni
- 2 cups shredded mozzarella cheese
- 1 (14 ounce) can pizza sauce

DIRECTIONS

1. Preheat oven to 375 degrees F (190 degrees C).
2. On a large baking sheet, pinch the 8 crescent roll dough triangles into 4 rectangles. Layer each rectangle with 6 slices of pepperoni and even amounts of mozzarella cheese. Roll tightly lengthwise and slice each into 4 or more pieces.
3. Bake in the preheated oven until golden brown, about 12 minutes. Serve with pizza sauce for dipping.

GREEK PENNE AND CHICKEN

Servings: 4 | Prep: 20m | Cooks: 30m | Total: 50m

NUTRITION FACTS

Calories: 684.7 | Carbohydrates: 96.2g | Protein: 47g | Cholesterol: 94mg

INGREDIENTS

- 1 (16 ounce) package penne pasta
- 1/2 cup crumbled feta cheese
- 1 1/2 tablespoons butter
- 3 tablespoons chopped fresh parsley
- 1/2 cup chopped red onion
- 2 tablespoons lemon juice
- 2 cloves garlic, minced
- 1 teaspoon dried oregano
- 1 pound skinless, boneless chicken breast halves - cut into bite-size pieces
- salt to taste
- 1 (14 ounce) can artichoke hearts in water
- ground black pepper to taste
- 1 tomato, chopped

DIRECTIONS

1. In a large pot with boiling salted water cook penne pasta until al dente. Drain.
2. Meanwhile, in a large skillet over medium-high heat melt butter, add onion and garlic and cook for 2 minutes. Add chopped chicken and continue cooking, stirring occasionally until golden brown, about 5 to 6 minutes.
3. Reduce heat to medium- low. Drain and chop artichoke hearts and add them, chopped tomato, feta cheese, fresh parsley, lemon juice, dried oregano, and drained penne pasta to the large skillet. Cook until heated through, about 2 to 3 minutes.
4. Season with salt and ground black pepper. Serve warm.

FRESH TOMATO SALSA

Servings: 4 | Prep: 10m | Cooks: 1h | Total: 1h10m | Additional: 1h

NUTRITION FACTS

Calories: 51 | Carbohydrates: 9.7g | Fat: 0.2g | Protein: 2.1g | Cholesterol: 0mg

INGREDIENTS

- 3 tomatoes, chopped

- 1/2 cup chopped fresh cilantro
- 1/2 cup finely diced onion
- 1 teaspoon salt
- 5 serrano chiles, finely chopped
- 2 teaspoons lime juice

DIRECTIONS

1. In a medium bowl, stir together tomatoes, onion, chili peppers, cilantro, salt, and lime juice. Chill for one hour in the refrigerator before serving.

JAY'S JERK CHICKEN

Servings: 4 | Prep: 15m | Cooks: 30m | Total: 4h45m | Additional: 4h

NUTRITION FACTS

Calories: 384.8 | Carbohydrates: 15.4g | Protein: 39.2g | Cholesterol: 96.9mg

INGREDIENTS

- 6 green onions, chopped
- 2 tablespoons brown sugar
- 1 onion, chopped
- 1 tablespoon chopped fresh thyme
- 1 jalapeno pepper, seeded and minced
- 1/2 teaspoon ground cloves
- 3/4 cup soy sauce
- 1/2 teaspoon ground nutmeg
- 1/2 cup distilled white vinegar
- 1/2 teaspoon ground allspice
- 1/4 cup vegetable oil
- 1 1/2 pounds skinless, boneless chicken breast halves

DIRECTIONS

1. In a food processor or blender, combine the green onions, onion, jalapeno pepper, soy sauce, vinegar, vegetable oil, brown sugar, thyme, cloves, nutmeg and allspice. Mix for about 15 seconds.
2. Place the chicken in a medium bowl, and coat with the marinade. Refrigerate for 4 to 6 hours, or overnight.
3. Preheat grill for high heat.
4. Lightly oil grill grate. Cook chicken on the prepared grill 6 to 8 minutes, until juices run clear.

COCONUT CURRY TOFU

Servings: 6 | Prep: 25m | Cooks: 15m | Total: 40m

NUTRITION FACTS

Calories: 232 | Carbohydrates: 16.9g | Fat: 13.2g | Protein: 16.5g | Cholesterol: 0mg

INGREDIENTS

- 2 bunches green onions
- 1 pound firm tofu, cut into 3/4 inch cubes
- 1 (14 ounce) can light coconut milk
- 4 roma (plum) tomatoes, chopped
- 1/4 cup soy sauce, divided
- 1 yellow bell pepper, thinly sliced
- 1/2 teaspoon brown sugar
- 4 ounces fresh mushrooms, chopped
- 1 1/2 teaspoons curry powder
- 1/4 cup chopped fresh basil
- 1 teaspoon minced fresh ginger
- 4 cups chopped bok choy
- 2 teaspoons chile paste
- salt to taste

DIRECTIONS

1. Remove white parts of green onions, and finely chop. Chop greens into 2 inch pieces.
2. In a large heavy skillet over medium heat, mix coconut milk, 3 tablespoons soy sauce, brown sugar, curry powder, ginger, and chile paste. Bring to a boil.
3. Stir tofu, tomatoes, yellow pepper, mushrooms, and finely chopped green onions into the skillet. Cover, and cook 5 minutes, stirring occasionally. Mix in basil and bok choy. Season with salt and remaining soy sauce. Continue cooking 5 minutes, or until vegetables are tender but crisp. Garnish with remaining green onion.

PORK CHOPS WITH FRESH TOMATO, ONION, GARLIC, AND FETA

Servings: 4 | Prep: 15m | Cooks: 20m | Total: 35m

NUTRITION FACTS

Calories: 452 | Carbohydrates: 34.1g | Fat: 17.9g | Protein: 40.7g | Cholesterol: 113mg

INGREDIENTS

- 2 tablespoons olive oil, divided
- garlic powder to taste
- 1 large onion, halved and thinly sliced
- 1/2 pint red grape tomatoes, halved
- 4 pork loin chops, 1 inch thick
- 1/2 pint yellow grape tomatoes, halved
- salt to taste
- 3 cloves garlic, diced
- black pepper to taste
- 2 1/2 teaspoons balsamic vinegar
- 1 tablespoon dried basil
- 4 ounces feta cheese, crumbled

DIRECTIONS

1. Heat 1 tablespoon oil in a skillet over medium heat. Stir in the onion and cook until golden brown. Set aside.
2. Heat 1/2 tablespoon oil in the skillet. Season pork chops with salt, pepper, and garlic powder, and place in the skillet. Cook to desired doneness. Set aside and keep warm.
3. Heat remaining oil in the skillet. Return onions to skillet, and stir in tomatoes, garlic, and basil. Cook and stir about 3 minutes, until tomatoes are tender. Mix in balsamic vinegar, and season with salt and pepper. Top chops with the onion and tomato mixture, and sprinkle with feta cheese to serve.

FETA CHICKEN

Servings: 6 | Prep: 15m | Cooks: 30m | Total: 45m

NUTRITION FACTS

Calories: 223.8 | Carbohydrates: 4.6g | Protein: 32g | Cholesterol: 93.7mg

INGREDIENTS

- 6 skinless, boneless chicken breast halves
- 6 ounces tomato basil feta cheese, crumbled
- 1/4 cup Italian-style dry bread crumbs, divided

DIRECTIONS

1. Preheat oven to 350 degrees F (175 degrees C). Lightly grease a 9x13 inch baking dish.
2. Place chicken breasts between 2 pieces of waxed paper. Gently pound chicken with flat side of meat mallet or rolling pin until about 1/4 inch thick; remove wax paper. Place 1 ounce of feta cheese in the center of each chicken breast, and fold in half.
3. Spread 2 tablespoons bread crumbs in the bottom of the prepared baking dish. Arrange chicken in the dish, and top with remaining bread crumbs.

4. Bake 25 to 30 minutes in the preheated oven, or until chicken is no longer pink and juices run clear.

ASIAN COCONUT RICE

Servings: 4 | Prep: 5m | Cooks: 20m | Total: 25m

NUTRITION FACTS

Calories: 453 | Carbohydrates: 61.4g | Fat: 20.9g | Protein: 6.8g | Cholesterol: 0mg

INGREDIENTS

- 1 (14 ounce) can coconut milk
- 1 pinch salt
- 1 1/4 cups water
- 1 1/2 cups uncooked jasmine rice
- 1 teaspoon sugar

DIRECTIONS

1. In a saucepan, combine coconut milk, water, sugar, and salt. Stir until sugar is dissolved. Stir in rice. Bring to a boil over medium heat. Cover, reduce heat, and simmer 18 to 20 minutes, until rice is tender.

BAKED COCONUT SHRIMP

Servings: 4 | Prep: 15m | Cooks: 15m | Total: 30m

NUTRITION FACTS

Calories: 310 | Carbohydrates: 29.3g | Fat: 11.4g | Protein: 22.5g | Cholesterol: 173mg

INGREDIENTS

- 1 pound large shrimp, peeled and deveined
- 3/4 teaspoon cayenne pepper
- 1/3 cup cornstarch
- 2 cups flaked sweetened coconut
- 1 teaspoon salt
- 3 egg whites, beaten until foamy

DIRECTIONS

1. Preheat an oven to 400 degrees F (200 degrees C). Lightly coat a baking sheet with cooking spray.
2. Rinse and dry shrimp with paper towels. Mix cornstarch, salt, and cayenne pepper in a shallow bow; pour coconut flakes in a separate shallow bowl. Working with one shrimp at a time, dredge it in the

cornstarch mixture, then dip it in the egg white, and roll it in the coconut, making sure to coat the shrimp well. Place on the prepared baking sheet, and repeat with the remaining shrimp.
3. Bake the shrimp until they are bright pink on the outside and the meat is no longer transparent in the center and the coconut is browned, 15 to 20 minutes, flipping the shrimp halfway through.

BREAKFAST PIES

Servings: 10 | Prep: 20m | Cooks: 20m | Total: 40m

NUTRITION FACTS

Calories: 247 | Carbohydrates: 15.8g | Fat: 15.7g | Protein: 10.5g | Cholesterol: 82mg

INGREDIENTS

- 3/4 pound breakfast sausage
- 3 eggs, beaten
- 1/8 cup minced onion
- 3 tablespoons milk
- 1/8 cup minced green bell pepper
- 1/2 cup shredded Colby-Monterey Jack cheese
- 1 (12 ounce) can refrigerated biscuit dough

DIRECTIONS

1. Preheat oven to 400 degrees F (200 degrees C).
2. In a large, deep skillet over medium-high heat, combine sausage, onion and green pepper. Cook until sausage is evenly brown. Drain, crumble, and set aside.
3. Separate the dough into 10 individual biscuits. Flatten each biscuit out, then line the bottom and sides of 10 muffin cups. Evenly distribute sausage mixture between the cups. Mix together the eggs and milk, and divide between the cups. Sprinkle tops with shredded cheese.
4. Bake in preheated oven for 18 to 20 minutes, or until filling is set.

SALMON PATTIES

Servings: 5 | Prep: 15m | Cooks: 10m | Total: 25m

NUTRITION FACTS

Calories: 224 | Carbohydrates: 9g | Fat: 10.4g | Protein: 22.3g | Cholesterol: 74mg

INGREDIENTS

- 1 (14.75 ounce) can canned salmon
- 1/2 cup seasoned dry bread crumbs
- 1 egg
- 1 tablespoon olive oil

- 1/4 cup chopped onion

DIRECTIONS

1. Drain and reserve liquid from salmon. Mix egg, onion, bread crumbs and salmon together.
2. Make into patties. If mixture is too dry to form into patties, add reserved liquid from salmon.
3. In a frying pan, heat olive oil. Place patties in pan. Brown on each side, turning gently. Drain on paper towels and serve.

CHICKEN BREASTS WITH LIME SAUCE
Servings: 4 | Prep: 15m | Cooks: 15m | Total: 30m

NUTRITION FACTS

Calories: 454.5 | Carbohydrates: 15.3g | Protein: 30.7g | Cholesterol: 164.2mg

INGREDIENTS

- 4 skinless, boneless chicken breast halves - pounded to 1/4 inch thickness
- 1 lime, juiced
- 1 egg, beaten
- 6 tablespoons butter
- 2/3 cup dry bread crumbs
- 1 teaspoon minced fresh chives
- 2 tablespoons olive oil
- 1/2 teaspoon dried dill weed

DIRECTIONS

1. Coat chicken breasts with egg, and dip in bread crumbs. Place on a wire rack, and allow to dry for about 10 minutes.
2. Heat olive oil in a large skillet over medium heat. Place chicken into the skillet, and fry for 3 to 5 minutes on each side. Remove to a platter, and keep warm.
3. Drain grease from the skillet, and squeeze in lime juice. Cook over low heat until it boils. Add butter, and stir until melted. Season with chives and dill. Spoon sauce over chicken, and serve immediately.

SIMPLE MACARONI AND CHEESE
Servings: 4 | Prep: 10m | Cooks: 20m | Total: 30m

NUTRITION FACTS

Calories: 630 | Carbohydrates: 55g | Fat: 33.6g | Protein: 26.5g | Cholesterol: 100mg

INGREDIENTS

- 1 (8 ounce) box elbow macaroni
- ground black pepper to taste
- 1/4 cup butter
- 2 cups milk
- 1/4 cup all-purpose flour
- 2 cups shredded Cheddar cheese
- 1/2 teaspoon salt

DIRECTIONS

1. Bring a large pot of lightly salted water to a boil. Cook elbow macaroni in the boiling water, stirring occasionally until cooked through but firm to the bite, 8 minutes. Drain.
2. Melt butter in a saucepan over medium heat; stir in flour, salt, and pepper until smooth, about 5 minutes. Slowly pour milk into butter-flour mixture while continuously stirring until mixture is smooth and bubbling, about 5 minutes. Add Cheddar cheese to milk mixture and stir until cheese is melted, 2 to 4 minutes.
3. Fold macaroni into cheese sauce until coated.

CREAMED CHIPPED BEEF ON TOAST

Servings: 4 | Prep: 10m | Cooks: 10m | Total: 20m

NUTRITION FACTS

Calories: 197 | Carbohydrates: 8.8g | Fat: 8.7g | Protein: 20.9g | Cholesterol: 67mg

INGREDIENTS

- 2 tablespoons butter
- 1 (8 ounce) jar dried beef
- 2 tablespoons all-purpose flour
- 1 pinch cayenne pepper
- 1 1/2 cups warm milk

DIRECTIONS

1. In a medium saucepan over low heat, melt butter. Whisk in flour all at once to form a roux. Whisk in milk, a little at a time, increase heat to medium-high, and cook, stirring, until thickened. Bring to a boil, stir in beef and cayenne, heat through and serve over toast.

GRILLED SAUSAGE WITH POTATOES AND GREEN BEANS

Servings: 4 | Prep: 25m | Cooks: 20m | Total: 45m

NUTRITION FACTS

Calories: 544 | Carbohydrates: 21.3g | Fat: 38.4g | Protein: 28.3g | Cholesterol: 80mg

INGREDIENTS

- 3/4 pound fresh green beans, trimmed and halved
- 1 teaspoon ground black pepper
- 1/2 pound red potatoes, quartered
- 1 teaspoon vegetable oil
- 1 large onion, sliced
- 1 teaspoon butter
- 1 pound smoked sausage, cut into 1 inch pieces
- 1/3 cup water
- 1 teaspoon salt

DIRECTIONS

1. Preheat an outdoor grill for high heat.
2. On a large sheet of foil, place the green beans, red potatoes, onion, and sausage. Season with salt and pepper, sprinkle with oil, and top with butter. Tightly seal foil around the ingredients, leaving only a small opening. Pour water into the opening, and seal.
3. Place foil packet on the prepared grill. Cook 20 to 30 minutes, turning once, until sausage is browned and vegetables are tender.

KIELBASA WITH PEPPERS AND POTATOES

Servings: 6 | Prep: 10m | Cooks: 30m | Total: 40m

NUTRITION FACTS

Calories: 404 | Carbohydrates: 36.1g | Fat: 23.2g | Protein: 13.3g | Cholesterol: 50mg

INGREDIENTS

- 1 tablespoon vegetable oil
- 1 red bell pepper, sliced
- 1 (16 ounce) package smoked kielbasa sausage, diced
- 1 yellow bell pepper, sliced
- 6 medium red potatoes, diced

DIRECTIONS

1. Heat the oil in a saucepan over medium heat. Place kielbasa and potatoes in the saucepan. Cover, and cook 25 minutes, stirring occasionally, until potatoes are tender.
2. Mix red bell pepper and yellow bell pepper into the saucepan, and continue cooking 5 minutes, until peppers are just tender.

GREEN BEAN AND MUSHROOM MEDLEY

Servings: 6 | Prep: 20m | Cooks: 15m | Total: 35m

NUTRITION FACTS

Calories: 103 | Carbohydrates: 7.7g | Fat: 7.9g | Protein: 1.9g | Cholesterol: 20mg

INGREDIENTS

- 1/2 pound fresh green beans, cut into 1-inch lengths
- 1 teaspoon salt
- 2 carrots, cut into thick strips
- 1/2 teaspoon seasoned salt
- 1/4 cup butter
- 1/4 teaspoon garlic salt
- 1 onion, sliced
- 1/4 teaspoon white pepper
- 1/2 pound fresh mushrooms, sliced

DIRECTIONS

1. Place green beans and carrots in 1 inch of boiling water. Cover, and cook until tender but still firm. Drain.
2. Melt butter in a large skillet over medium heat. Saute onions and mushrooms until almost tender. Reduce heat, cover, and simmer 3 minutes. Stir in green beans, carrots, salt, seasoned salt, garlic salt, and white pepper. Cover, and cook for 5 minutes over medium heat.

SMOKY GRILLED PORK CHOPS

Servings: 4 | Prep: 10m | Cooks: 25m | Total: 55m | Additional: 20m

NUTRITION FACTS

Calories: 254 | Carbohydrates: 5.4g | Fat: 14.3g | Protein: 25g | Cholesterol: 66mg

INGREDIENTS

- 1 tablespoon seasoned salt (such as LAWRY'S)
- 1 tablespoon ground paprika
- 1 teaspoon ground black pepper
- 2 teaspoons Worcestershire sauce
- 1 tablespoon garlic powder
- 1 teaspoon liquid smoke flavoring
- 1 tablespoon onion powder
- 4 bone-in pork chops (1/2 to 3/4 inch thick)

DIRECTIONS

1. Preheat an outdoor grill for medium heat, and lightly oil the grate.
2. In a bowl, mix together the seasoned salt, black pepper, garlic powder, onion powder, paprika, Worcestershire sauce, and smoke flavoring until thoroughly combined. Rinse pork chops, and sprinkle the wet chops on both sides with the spice mixture. With your hands, massage the spice rub into the meat; allow to stand for 10 minutes.
3. Grill the chops over indirect heat until no longer pink inside, about 12 minutes per side. An instant-read thermometer should read at least 145 degrees F (63 degrees C). Allow chops to stand for 10 more minutes before serving.

CHILI DOG CASSEROLE

Servings: 10 | Prep: 15m | Cooks: 30m | Total: 45m

NUTRITION FACTS

Calories: 491 | Carbohydrates: 39.4g | Fat: 28.8g | Protein: 19.7g | Cholesterol: 62mg

INGREDIENTS

- 2 (15 ounce) cans chili with beans
- 10 (8 inch) flour tortillas
- 1 (16 ounce) package beef frankfurters
- 1 (8 ounce) package Cheddar cheese, shredded

DIRECTIONS

1. Preheat oven to 425 degrees F (220 degrees C).
2. Spread 1 can of chili and beans in the bottom of a 9x13 inch baking dish. Roll up franks inside tortillas and place in baking dish, seam side down, on top of chili and bean 'bed'. Top with remaining can of chili and beans, and sprinkle with cheese.
3. Cover baking dish with aluminum foil, and bake at 425 degrees F (220 degrees C) for 30 minutes.

BEST TUNA MELT (NEW JERSEY DINER STYLE)

Servings: 4 | Prep: 10m | Cooks: 5m | Total: 15m

NUTRITION FACTS

Calories: 484 | Carbohydrates: 22.1g | Fat: 28.4g | Protein: 34.8g | Cholesterol: 76mg

INGREDIENTS

- 2 (5 ounce) cans tuna, drained
- 1 pinch salt
- 1/4 cup mayonnaise
- 1 pinch freshly ground black pepper
- 1/4 cup finely chopped celery
- 4 slices seedless rye bread
- 1 1/2 tablespoons finely chopped onion
- 8 slices ripe tomato
- 1 tablespoon chopped parsley
- 8 slices Swiss cheese
- 3/4 teaspoon red wine vinegar
- paprika, for garnish

DIRECTIONS

1. Preheat the oven broiler.
2. In a bowl, mix the tuna, mayonnaise, celery, onion, parsley, and vinegar. Season with salt and pepper.
3. Place the rye bread slices on a baking sheet, and broil 1 minute in the preheated oven, until lightly toasted. Remove from heat, and spread with the tuna salad. Place 1 cheese slice over the tuna salad on each piece of bread, layer with a tomato slice, and top with remaining cheese slices.
4. Return layered bread to the preheated oven, and broil 3 to 5 minutes, until cheese is melted.

GINGER VEGGIE STIR-FRY

Servings: 6 | Prep: 25m | Cooks: 15m | Total: 40m

NUTRITION FACTS

Calories: 119 | Carbohydrates: 8g | Fat: 9.3g | Protein: 2.2g | Cholesterol: 0mg

INGREDIENTS

- 1 tablespoon cornstarch
- 3/4 cup julienned carrots
- 1 1/2 cloves garlic, crushed

- 1/2 cup halved green beans
- 2 teaspoons chopped fresh ginger root, divided
- 2 tablespoons soy sauce
- 1/4 cup vegetable oil, divided
- 2 1/2 tablespoons water
- 1 small head broccoli, cut into florets
- 1/4 cup chopped onion
- 1/2 cup snow peas
- 1/2 tablespoon salt

DIRECTIONS

1. In a large bowl, blend cornstarch, garlic, 1 teaspoon ginger, and 2 tablespoons vegetable oil until cornstarch is dissolved. Mix in broccoli, snow peas, carrots, and green beans, tossing to lightly coat.
2. Heat remaining 2 tablespoons oil in a large skillet or wok over medium heat. Cook vegetables in oil for 2 minutes, stirring constantly to prevent burning. Stir in soy sauce and water. Mix in onion, salt, and remaining 1 teaspoon ginger. Cook until vegetables are tender but still crisp.

CHICKEN FIESTA SALAD

Servings: 4 | Prep: 10m | Cooks: 30m | Total: 40m

NUTRITION FACTS

Calories: 310.8 | Carbohydrates: 42.2g | Protein: 23g | Cholesterol: 35.9mg

INGREDIENTS

- 2 skinless, boneless chicken breast halves
- 1/2 cup salsa
- 1 (1.27 ounce) packet dry fajita seasoning, divided
- 1 (10 ounce) package mixed salad greens
- 1 tablespoon vegetable oil
- 1 onion, chopped
- 1 (15 ounce) can black beans, rinsed and drained
- 1 tomato, cut into wedges
- 1 (11 ounce) can Mexican-style corn

DIRECTIONS

1. Rub chicken evenly with 1/2 the fajita seasoning. Heat the oil in a skillet over medium heat, and cook the chicken 8 minutes on each side, or until juices run clear; set aside.
2. In a large saucepan, mix beans, corn, salsa and other 1/2 of fajita seasoning. Heat over medium heat until warm.

3. Prepare the salad by tossing the greens, onion and tomato. Top salad with chicken and dress with the bean and corn mixture.

SPICY CHICKEN BREASTS

Servings: 4 | Prep: 15m | Cooks: 15m | Total: 30m

NUTRITION FACTS

Calories: 173 | Carbohydrates: 9.2g | Protein: 29.2g | Cholesterol: 68.4mg

INGREDIENTS

- 2 1/2 tablespoons paprika
- 1 tablespoon dried thyme
- 2 tablespoons garlic powder
- 1 tablespoon ground cayenne pepper
- 1 tablespoon salt
- 1 tablespoon ground black pepper
- 1 tablespoon onion powder
- 4 skinless, boneless chicken breast halves

DIRECTIONS

1. In a medium bowl, mix together the paprika, garlic powder, salt, onion powder, thyme, cayenne pepper, and ground black pepper. Set aside about 3 tablespoons of this seasoning mixture for the chicken; store the remainder in an airtight container for later use (for seasoning fish, meats, or vegetables).
2. Preheat grill for medium-high heat. Rub some of the reserved 3 tablespoons of seasoning onto both sides of the chicken breasts.
3. Lightly oil the grill grate. Place chicken on the grill, and cook for 6 to 8 minutes on each side, until juices run clear.

CHICKEN BREASTS WITH HERB BASTING SAUCE

Servings: 4 | Prep: 15m | Cooks: 45m | Total: 1h

NUTRITION FACTS

Calories: 391.5 | Carbohydrates: 1.1g | Protein: 45.1g | Cholesterol: 126.6mg

INGREDIENTS

- 3 tablespoons olive oil
- 1/4 teaspoon dried marjoram
- 1 tablespoon minced onion

- 1/2 teaspoon salt
- 1 clove crushed garlic
- 1/2 teaspoon ground black pepper
- 1 teaspoon dried thyme
- 1/8 teaspoon hot pepper sauce
- 1/2 teaspoon dried rosemary, crushed
- 4 bone-in chicken breast halves, with skin
- 1/4 teaspoon ground sage
- 1 1/2 tablespoons chopped fresh parsley

DIRECTIONS

1. Preheat oven to 425 degrees F (220 degrees C).
2. In a bowl, prepare the basting sauce by combining olive oil, onion, garlic, thyme, rosemary, sage, marjoram, salt, pepper, and hot pepper sauce.
3. Turn chicken breasts in sauce to coat thoroughly. Place skin side up in a shallow baking dish. Cover.
4. Roast at 425 degrees F (220 degrees C), basting occasionally with pan drippings, for about 35 to 45 minutes. Remove to warm platter, spoon pan juices over, and sprinkle with fresh parsley.

QUICK BRUSCHETTA CHICKEN BAKE

Servings: 6 | Prep: 20m | Cooks: 30m | Total: 50m

NUTRITION FACTS

Calories: 230 | Carbohydrates: 8.2g | Fat: 9.4g | Protein: 21.2g | Cholesterol: 41mg

INGREDIENTS

- 1 1/2 pounds skinless, boneless chicken breast halves - cubed
- 1 tablespoon minced garlic
- 1 teaspoon salt
- 1 (6 ounce) box chicken-flavored dry bread stuffing mix
- 1 (15 ounce) can diced tomatoes with juice
- 2 cups shredded mozzarella cheese
- 1/2 cup water
- 1 tablespoon Italian seasoning

DIRECTIONS

1. Preheat oven to 400 degrees F (200 degrees C). Spray a 9x13-inch glass baking dish with cooking spray.
2. Toss the cubed chicken with the salt in a large bowl. Place the chicken in a layer into the bottom of the baking dish. Stir together tomatoes, water, garlic, and stuffing mix in a large bowl; set aside to

soften. Sprinkle the cheese on top of the chicken, then sprinkle with the Italian seasoning. Spread the softened stuffing mixture on top.
3. Bake uncovered until the chicken cubes have turned white and are no longer pink in the center, about 30 minutes.

Milton Keynes UK
Ingram Content Group UK Ltd.
UKHW051540080724
445334UK00041B/1373